Schadenfreude:

The Little Book of Black Delights

Tim Lihoreau

First published 2011 by Elliott and Thompson Limited
27 John Street, London WC1N 2BX
www.eandtbooks.com

ISBN: 978-1-907642-37-1

Text © Tim Lihoreau 2011

9 8 7 6 5 4 3 2 1

A CIP catalogue record for this book is available from the British Library.

Printed and bound in the UK by TJ International

Typeset by PDQ
Cover designed by James Collins

For Suzanne and Pete – and the Moulin de Roche, the perfect writing place.

Foreword

To paraphrase an old line, I still don't quite know why my mother didn't make me a mornuntiaphiliac. Perhaps she didn't have the wool, so made me a purple tank top instead.

I am only partially joking. My mum always used to be an inveterate mornuntiaphiliac, a supreme mistress of this particularly dark art. Her skill with the extended, tortuously tantalizing, almost labyrinthine lead in, sometimes lasting several minutes and always culminating in the totally expected but somehow nevertheless shocking revelation of a friend's mortality, was second to none. As a party piece, it wasn't quite up there with playing the accordion or telling gags, but it formed a crucial part of my growing years.

Perhaps she would still be a mornuntiaphiliac today, if her mind didn't play such tricks on her. As to why she didn't pass this trait down to me, that got me thinking: we must all have our own *Schadenfreude* palette, a blotchy, mottled board which we use to occasionally dab our souls, not with vivid, fluorescent colours but with a scale of blacks and charcoals, sables and jets. On it, too, would be a wash of greys and slates: battleship grey, gunmetal grey, quartz grey and even the truly pit-dwelling arsenic grey.

So I decided to collect them. To admit to some of them, perhaps, but mainly to collate and christen them – each ambrosial bliss, each nectarious relish, each ravishing indulgence. Some, as you will see, are darker than others – fully-blown *Schadenfreude*, delighting in every nuance of another's *precise* misfortune. Others, though, are hardly dictionary-definition *Schadenfreude* at all but simply wicked pleasures. Yes, there is always some offshoot agony somewhere down the line, but it might be a distant by-product of what is merely a more personal, secret sin.

When scrambling around for a name, a little inky ribbon to bind them, I first thought it should be a Tao – a little 'Tao of *Schadenfreude*', if you like. After all, it could be said that these are the unacknowledged, private yins that sit beside our colourful, public yangs. We all occupy both of these spaces, but perhaps we don't always admit so readily to the yin's shade alongside the yang's light.

Admit to some, I said. So here goes. While in my youth there may certainly have been some self-preserving resistance to *Mornuntiaphilia*, I am pretty sure that one of my earliest childhood recollections is of a turpaphiliac neighbour, who took one look at me – despite being the shape of a space hopper now, back then I think I was already lanky while still in the cot – and said 'Lovely pram. Is that the Silver Cross Viceroy?' It may be a trick of the memory. Perhaps she was comparing me to some former colonial type she knew but I doubt it. Very few ever passed by our particular neck of Leeds.

As a student, I began to work at the local opera house, checking the tickets of the rich, the famous and the corporate. Call me a benedixophile if you like (and I will certainly admit to *Eboracophilia* since birth) but it was here that I first encountered *Priplaudophilia*. Set in the literal darkness of the orchestra, stalls were a seedbed of priplaudophiliac males (it always seemed to be men), each of them almost spring-loaded, baying to be the first to be able to ruin the moment.

Now? Now I am but a verophiliac, nothesophiliac libresophile with ruberinophiliac tendencies – but my deepest darkest joy, my most *schaden* of *Freudes*, has got to be *Mendicaphilia*.

And so.

How to use this book

I do love seeing that line in the front of books, today. Perhaps here it should say 1) open, 2) read, 3) laugh occasionally? and 4) simply delight. For this reason, I have not separated the book into its main genres (see below) but I have provided an index in order that you might dip in and delight. Perhaps even self-diagnose.

As far as suggestions go, had I organised this into sections, it would have almost certainly been in four:

~ the lavorophilias – the work delights
~ the vitaphilias – the daily life delights
~ the fornophilias – the sexual delights
~ the miscellophilias – the rest, including those concerned with recreation and entertainment

Lavorophilias are those most commonly observed or practised in the workplace, particularly the larger, more corporate arenas: try starting with common ones like the rather tart *Nodonophilia*. Vitaphilias are those for which we can probably all hold our hands up and embarrassingly try to 'high five' to: *Callidinfanophilia* is very common now, for example, as are *Nothesophilia* and *Infrenophilia*.

For those of a more stable disposition, the fornophilias offer up such pearls as *Maximentophilia* or *Coclearophilia*. There are more, but I am far too polite to point them out here. I'm sure you will find them if you seek them.

Finally, the miscellophilias. The rest, so to speak. Where to start here? Well, you could do worse than try the increasingly common *Vinoptophilia*; the childish delight of even *Nimbuphilia*; and who but a saint can resist *Tefamaphilia*?

However you light your way through the murky pages of this book, I do recommend you embrace your ebony raptures, your sooty spoils, your *Schadenfreudes*. We will all be the better for it.

Tim Lihoreau

Accugeophilia: delight in 'outing' a fake residential area.

To be fair to accugeophiles, quite how dark their philia is depends on how militant they choose to be when it comes to outing their victims. At its gentlest, this is hardly a philia at all and merely an attempt to prevent the spread of tosh, said to have started in the bowels of the 1980s. Back in those dark days, Streatham became St. Reatham and Battersea morphed into Lower Chelsea, so the accugeophile's work was much appreciated by all, not just themselves. Nowadays, however, like many things, its origins have become muddied and its methods argued over by ever more disparate branches of the same root cause. For most, though, this is a harmless, if a little shady, recreation, usually enjoyed verbally among friends who will recover. For example, 'I'm so sorry we're late. I set the sat nav for Hampstead borders, like you said, and it took us miles away. It was ages before we realised you meant Kentish town!'

[accuratus, accurate; geographia, geography]

§

Adverursophilia: delight in not knowing the answer to a question.

Very high up on the list of workplace delights is *Adverursophilia*. If all the dark circumstances that can fall into place do, this can not only prove one of the most piquant delicacies available to the lower office orders – the Production Plankton – in their daily pursuit of transient delights, but also bring some temporary sense of social justice. The subject, the adverursophiliac, often has to put in a substantial amount of groundwork for maximum joy. Key to their pleasure is the temporary amnesia, a general understanding by all involved that, at some point in the past, they did indeed know the answer to the question at the heart of the matter. Then, at the point of maximum potential embarrassment – The Golden Point* – when asked to supply a key piece of path-critical information, they simply utter the trigger phrase, which has brought down many a previously great middle manager: 'I'm sorry… I'm not with you?'

And so the game commences, with a phrase as deadly as it is telling: on one level it simply displays an apparent lack of understanding, but on another it implicitly says 'I am no longer on your side'. Lethal. Very often, the 'question' at the heart is not a question at all. It can be a call to verify, a signal to commence a pre-planned mini-presentation, or even the chance to demonstrate 'succession planning'. Most frequently, though, it is a simple question: 'Isn't that right, Ashley?' Cue a few seconds silence. 'Ashley?' More silence, then that trigger phrase: 'I'm sorry… I'm not with you?' BOOM! There it is. The beginning of the end. If the adverursophiliac has done enough groundwork – and let's be under no delusions, this is a risky business – then a boardroom coup may well be underway and one's boss has taken the first steps pell-mell down the emergency exit on the way to becoming one's former boss. As they say in the workplace, revenge is a dish best kept out of the minutes.

On a more everyday level, the adverursophile has merely won himself some much needed office comfort: it may be temporary, it may even be ultimately holing themselves below the water line, but it is joy in its truest sense. It might earn them some finite respect in terms of toilet graffiti or even a deliberately mismatched newspaper headline, extracted and mounted on the kitchen pinboard: 'I'd do the same all over again, says Ashley!' ripped from the *Daily Star*. A gem.

*see *How to Survive Your Boss*, work in progress, Tim Lihoreau

[adversus rursus, volte-face]

Adverviriophilia: delight in not recycling.

With a name deriving from the diametric opposite of green on the standard colour wheel, adverviriophiles are not, by any measure, anti-green. At least, not for 98 per cent of the time. They are not global-warming deniers nor shirkers of responsibility, either. It is just that, once in a while, as a treat for being so good, they award themselves this inky, honeyed pleasure, that of *shoving everything in together*. They allow themselves not to recycle. For one moment, as the planet sinks to new depths, they are walking on sunshine and, in the words of a certain 1980s popstar, don't it feel good! The sheer, albeit temporary, titillation of not having to separate their rubbish feels, for a moment, simply succulent and any thoughts of the Earth are limited to seeing it from space as they float in high orbit.

On the other hand, *Adverviriophilia luxa* – a delight in leaving the light on – can hit people when they are least expecting it, leaving them with a sneaking suspicion that, deep down, they are genuinely unreconstructed about this whole issue and that, maybe, they don't buy all this green stuff, after all. Why, for example, would they have had their hand poised easily over the light switch, their TV dinner in the other hand, only to find themselves smiling and choosing to leave the light on. Of course, there are simply people who do not '*do de simia*'* as the visionary Pliny once said.

One further strain exists – namely *Adverviriophilia otia*. This shady indulgence is enjoyed while on holiday – it can be in a villa, in a hotel, or simply while in another person's home, however temporarily – and one allows oneself the orgasmic delight of leaving everything on: TV, aircon, lights, as many items on charge as you could find plugs.

[adversus, opposite; viridis, green; do de simia, give a monkey's; otium, holiday]

☙

Alavellophilia: delight in spoiling a child's game when unseen.

The name of this philia reveals everything you need to know. It is derived from *ala* and *vello*: wings and pulling. Alavellophiliacs *do* exist, they *are* out there and they know who they are. As their name suggests, they were the ones who pulled the wings off insects when they were young. A tiny percentage of them do what they do to get their own back on a particularly irritating kid. Sadly, 99.9 per cent do not. If you know your partner is an alavellophiliac, you should take steps. Perhaps join a large number of time-consuming unpaid organisations (the chair of governors in a school is ideal). Also, try not to breed.

[ala, wings; vello, pull]

§

Aldarophilia: delight in putting it on expenses.

Britain's MPs have been responsible for giving the word 'expenses' a bad name. It should be noted that *Aldarophilia* is in no way associated with fiddling expenses. It is merely the animal delight in buying something in the knowledge that someone else is paying. No further twist need be added. One needn't buy a better model than one would have done. One needn't buy several at once. No, this is simply the dark delight in knowing that when it comes to the ultimate reckoning for this chicken in a basket and two glasses of Chianti enjoyed in the Leicester Premier

Inn one sad November night, the personal fortune which you are able to bequest to your offspring will not be affected. As definitions of *L'heure exquise* go, it's pretty damn close. Can a delight such as this ever pale with the knowledge that another person's loss (as in profit & loss) will be increased?

As with every yin, there is a yang. This is known as *Aldarophilia spirilia* and occurs when a lax attitude is adopted with regard to the filling in of one's expenses forms. Again, nothing sinister is at play here. It is merely the nature of modern work, in which 15-hour days are the norm and the time to complete expenses forms is redefined as 'free time'. Here, *Aldarophilia spirilia* sufferers find themselves so behind in their claims that they often find they are diverting money from their subsistence essentials simply in order to maintain their working lifestyle. In this instance, it is their bosses who enjoy the delights, treating them as akin to a monthly overdraft which bosses, if they are lucky, may never even have to pay off. This can happen with tax returns, too, in which case it is known as 'time in jail'.

[alius, other; dare, pay]

§

Amgaulophilia: delight in a love of French films, laboriously worn.

Amgaulophiliacs are not hard to spot. They are generally male, heavily into men's grooming products and don't first think of motorbikes when you say Kurosawa. If you want to self-diagnose, then for a clinching, almost medical, decider question, ask yourself if you are just as agitated about whether they will ever make another series of the Swedish version of *Wallander* as you are about the amount of media time given to global warming deniers. If the answer is yes, then you may unwittingly be an amgaulophiliac. In a world where *Newsnight Review* is not yet available on the National Health, 'amgaulos' tend to wear their love of French film much as a cricket umpire wears jerseys. They delight in dropping French names the way others might drop Hs, and entire scene references which go so far over others' heads they need a flight plan. If you think Pagnol is what Parisians take for their migraine, then you are not a sufferer.

Amgaulophilia tempesta is a subsidiary condition where the subject waits in silence as you discuss the latest Harry Potter film, only to strike – eyes heavenwards and a rictus grin contorting their features – with the casual observation that the final scene in the Hogwarts entrance hall '…was clearly referencing *La Double Vie de Veronique*, and, incidentally, there's a season of Truffaut on at the Screen in the Spleen* at the moment'. Definitely someone who delights in only enjoying their films in seasons.

*Hampstead's trendiest cinema built from a refurbished hospital operating theatre.

[amo, love; gaul, France; tempesta, season]

Ampropaquophilia: delight in abstaining from something.

This is less dark and certainly less sinister than *Tudolophilia* (qv); ampropaquophiles would, in less enlightened times, simply have been labelled 'smug' and conveniently locked away from the general public. With what some might see as the unfortunate lack of a suitable substitute for Bedlam, today ampropaquophiles are encouraged to assimilate into most areas of polite society (some working men's clubs still refuse them entry), and their smugness is tolerated by most.

The ampropaquophile's pleasure is derived from accumulating self-righteousness, an ironic black delight based on the denial of delight itself. Each new relinquished recreation is greeted as a sacrifice to be savoured, as if they are members of the *Opus Dei* branch of life itself. The mantra will be familiar to all. Sugar doughnut? 'Not for me.' Glass of wine? 'Not for me.' Songs of love? 'Not for me.' (A related but wholly separate strain is that of *Tudolophilia curratomba*, which is the delight in witnessing someone fall off the wagon and 'give up their giving up', as it were.) This is a delicious philia, made all the more delectable if it was something you would have loved to have given up yourself.

[amo, love; pro, before; pascha, Easter]

Antevoluptophilia: delight in 'inadvertently' revealing the plot of a film.

The inverted commas should be noted. This is obviously a bit of a misnomer and not inadvertent at all. Most antevoluptophiliacs just want to spoil the fun. It's that simple. It may seem like an accident on so many occasions but it rarely is. *Antevoluptophilia continua* sufferers do it in stages, as each section of the film unfurls, to maximise their own pleasure. Usually, they give morsels of plot away with lines like 'Oh, and see what he does with that key, because it's important when they find Carlo's body, later'. Of course, as they sink back into their popcorn-strewn seat, they know all too well that Carlo is alive and well and wandering around the screen. This can happen up to a further five times during an average movie. Up to ten in *Le Chagrin et le Pitié*. There is only one way to spoil an antevoluptophile's fun and that is to take them to a Jean-Luc Godard movie (or any film that has ever kicked off the Venice Biennale), where there is too little plot to reveal.

[ante, before; voluptas, delight; continua, continuous]

Aviaphilia: delight in winding up friends' children before leaving.

Along with gin and Grandad, this is sometimes referred to as 'grandma's delight', due to the high number of sufferers in this category. Nevertheless, it is practised by many other demographics, including the childless,

the homosexual and the middle-management virgin. Similar in outlook to chaophiliacs (qv), aviaphiliacs tend to treat children as if they are a set of those walking teeth toys: simply wind them up, put them down and laugh your head off as they annoy the hell out of everybody. Grandmas take a further strange view. When they themselves were young, the rules were there to be obeyed. Now, along with the world records for earliest drink of the day and most insensitive personal comment, they are there to be broken. With Saint Jenny of Joseph as their patron, they spit, wear purple and take an ageing delight in encouraging their grandchildren to simply let go. Then they leave their offspring behind to cope with a smiling, screaming, shouting, giant E number. Which, in a parallel reality, is a line from a Cliff Richard song.
[avia, grandmother]

Benedixophilia: delight in
baiting a posh person.

Interestingly enough, the *bene dix* of this philia is not the 'well-spoken' posh person you might think in the definition. It in fact refers to the act of posh-person baiting itself, an act historically thought to involve some very 'well-said' phrases by dint of nature. *Benedixophilia* goes far beyond simple mockery and repeated phrases. Most experts in this dark art thrive on the subliminal reference, hoping for at least the silver-standard goal of the quizzical look, denoting an uncertainty in the victim about whether a dig has just been made or not. 'Do you ever watch *The One Show?*' was one I noted down in the field recently, a gentle sideswipe at how often the word 'one' was used instead of 'I'. Other methods include what Arthur Mullard called 'crunching juxtapositions'* when one deliberately butts up a slice of 'us' against a slice of 'them' in conversation. Thus:

'My driver tells me that petrol has gone through the roof!'

'Really? My driver tells me it's now £1.70 to go just one stop!'

Eventually, many chronic benedixophiliacs find that the simple pleasures become bland all too soon, and one seeks what Mullard terms 'posh spice' – a *famous* posh person or one who has presented a nature programme at the very least. Ben Fogle is often seen as a target, but the jewel in the crown would be a 'Bullingdon' MP. 'Everybody likes a bit o' Bully', as famous benedixophile Jim Bowen was wont to say.

Living the Lie – Humble Essays on the Essential Tortures of High Birth by Baron Arthur de la Mullarde of Ravenshall, Ravenshall Manor Press. If you have never read this book, let me recommend it. It is the seminal book in which 'Arfur Mullard' as his public knew him, essentially 'came out' and revealed his previously hidden, privileged background. The chapters detailing his beatings at Uppingham – and how he administered them – are beyond powerful.

[bene, well, dicere to speak]

Boretophilia: delight in having a good memory.

Just to explain, the full definition should read 'delight in having a good memory when all around you are losing theirs'. Boretophiliacs take their pleasures from sourcing, from within their own age group,* those who simply can't remember things as well as themselves. They will delight in filling in words in conversational gaps that even *Just a Minute* wouldn't have buzzed for. Their standard joy, though, is to demonstrate great memory immediately after their friend's demonstration of bad or perhaps, for greater discomfort, when the subject of 'bad memory' has just been humbly confessed. Some veterans will even walk a few paces behind friends who wander into other rooms, in order to stop behind them when they pause and say 'Your glasses, you came in here for your glasses!' The main thing to remember about *Boretophilia* is… [Note to self: Remember to finish this before going to publication.]

*It has to be from the same age group or lower. The working title for the game show 'Are you smarter than a ten year old?' was allegedly 'Would a ten year old know what I did with my keys?'

[bonum, good; retinentia, memory]

Caetumalbophilia: delight in checking that another team lost before you check your own team won.

This is a delight that will usually show itself between

the ages of five and 18, and the cases of late-onset *Caetumalbophilia* are few and far between. Named after the author's personal delight in checking that Chelsea have lost prior to checking that Leeds have won, it is often an irrational joy in which the original parameters of the pleasure have changed and yet the delight still lingers. Nothing, for example, can prevent the author raising a smile when the pricy team of Russian-funded foreigners go down (the lowlier the conquerors, of course, the greater the joy) despite the fact that the team he learnt to truly despise as an impressionable, Chopper-loving Spacehopper owner were a world apart. Nevertheless, the philia is still there. When he checks in 2012 to find that Chelsea have lost and Leeds have won, in his heart he feels the *Freude* of Bremner, Giles, Lorimer *et al* trouncing Osgood and Bonetti. It's like Skywalker destroying the Death Star.

[caerulus, blue: albus, white]

ও

Cadangliophilia: delight at a British sporting defeat.

A hardy perennial delight on these shores, *Cadangliophilia* is most common in its 'trophy' strain, *Cadangliophilia wynma* (delight at a tennis defeat). This is seasonal, occurring around June each year at the first sight of what are perversely called 'British hopefuls' lining up for their first matches at Wimbledon. Other strains exist, however, such as *Cadangliophilia globa* (football), *Candangliophilia scortea-salix* (cricket) and even the acute *Cadangliophilia scortea-salix 'Cinis'*, a specific 'Ashes' sub-strain. Overall, this delight is generally led from the press box but it can enter the workplace too. Pre-Wimbledon, amidst the traditional public bout of amnesia, before full failure has become apparent, a cruel belief sets in. Maybe this time? Before the *anglus pignus* (token Brit) has met their Dunkirk, newspapers lead the frenzy with suggestions to rename the hill at Wimbledon; Henman Hill becomes Murray Mount and so forth. The cadangliophile might publicly consider suggesting Everest, seeing as most Britons' journey to the top is usually followed by a swift descent before ending up in the dead zone.

Catchphrases include: 'Don't get me wrong, I'd LOVE him to win this year, I genuinely would!'

[cado, failure; Anglia, Brit.; wynma, Wimbledon; globus, ball; scorteus, leather; salix, willow; cinis, ashes]

ς

Calicurrophilia: delight in the team that knocked you out being beaten.

Etymologists, looking at this one in the future, might try to tie its meaning to some sort of excess of delight, in which 'the cup runneth over'. Sadly, the truth behind this philia is much more mundane. This is the pleasure taken when the party that conquered you is finally conquered themselves and derives from the annual popular debacle that is the FA Cup.

Many a supporter has found themselves in the car at 4.45 p.m. on a Saturday afternoon, punching the air at *Final Score*, as they become calicurrophiles for the first time on hearing that their nemesis was hammered four-nil. At home. Psychologists have also adopted the etymology for *Calicurrophilia amora*, in which the subject delights in finding out that their former lover, who dumped them by phone, has been dumped themselves. On Facebook. Ambrosial!

[calix, cup: curro, run]

§

Callidinfanophilia: delight in the possession of a bright child.

Not to be confused with – because it is totally different from – *Stultinfanophilia* (qv). Callidinfanophiles delight in simple pleasures: intelligence, talent and a rigorous hothouse system that has been in place since before their children were born. It comes in three distinct hues: *Callidinfanophilia vicaria*, *Callidinfanophilia nova pecunia* and *Callidinfanophilia traditus*. It is interesting to note that, were three pleasure-seekers from each strain to meet, they would find that their delight paths rarely crossed. *Callidinfanophilia traditus* is the oldest delight, affecting mainly the landed gentry. Practitioners tend to delight less in the brightness of the child and more in the continuation of a tradition of brightness stemming back to their ancestors, who helped Noah with the finer engineering details for the Ark. Catchphrases include 'It wasn't really a case of could we afford to send her to Benenden, it was rather could we afford *not* to ...'.

The *Nova pecunia* strain affects its subjects in the opposite way, with parents, particularly fathers, enjoying all manner of dark delicacies from their offspring's obvious genius which ensued from them 'having had things I never 'ad, Son' (these last seven words are uttered in a Yorkshire accent).

Most virulent of the three is the *Vicaria* strain, in which the parents revel in the achievements of the children themselves. These are the types who have to be pulled back into their seats when they stand up and punch the air with a whooped 'Back of the net!' at prize givings. Occasionally, they might also modify their language to take on the current version of youth-speak, even changing the 'you' to 'I' (having briefly dallied with 'we') when talking about projected results. That is, before it all got out of hand, it might have been 'You must put aside time to revise, yes?' Then, when things were mild, it was 'We need that B in French, remember?' Now, fullly-blown, it mutates into: 'Yes! ... I've got 98 per cent for that essay on the Spanish Civil War. I'll ring Maria and see if she fancies a drink'. At this point, with the other parent looking on with a mixture of worry and fear, it is up to the offspring to remind their parent that *they* got 98 per cent and Maria is *their* girlfriend.

[callido, brainy; infans, child; pecunia, money; traditus, tradition]

Calxantephilia: delight in deliberately stepping on the heel of the person in front.

Among Cambridge University lecturers, this became known for a time in the 1920s as 'Seeing the arrow on to Achilles' and is thought to be the reason senior staff were originally given rights to cross the lawned areas of the quad, rights they still hold today. Some lecturers found their paths so tediously delayed by students and tourists alike that they simply 'helped' the strolling masses on their way with a little trip. Today, it is rarely seen in the cloisters, but the aforementioned tourists do still find themselves at the heart of this black delight, as it is now most often practised in major shopping streets, places of interest and the queue of Madame Tussaud's.

The rules of *Calxantephilia* are said to be more complex than chess, with various ways and means of attack and defence. Most people who enjoy a little 'Achillean Amusement' do so with the standard 'Bader Defence*', which is to deny not just all knowledge but even the faintest hint of possibility that the offending foot on the back of the heel could have belonged to you. So much for the convoluted defences. The pleasures of the calxantephiliac are much easier to discern. Some of the most irritating people ever to have trod the soil are those who have done so at a truly funereal pace while all around them bustle. They are often tourists, sometimes lovers, occasionally TV news reporters doing walks to camera. The elderly, it should be noted, do not count, their pace of life being deemed a lesson to us all.

*It is unnecessary to delve into how this manoeuvre gained its name, save to say it was a truly baffling *cause célèbre* in the RAF during the war, which, thankfully, never came to civilian court. Other principal manoeuvres include the Lady Hamilton (involves motioning to your feet in a silent attempt to imply that your dress means that it could not possibly have been you), the George Hamilton IV (doff the cap and say 'Ma'am' in a US accent before moving on whistling a tune) and the Neil Hamilton (simply smile like a loon as if it never happened). History is unclear as to why so many calx-defences are named after Hamiltons.

[calx, heel; ante, in front]]

§

Calxluxophilia: delight in stealing the limelight.

Calxluxophiles will never, it's probably true, make good support actors. Or colleagues. Or spouses. They simply love to upstage too much. Whether they are settling an old score in an office boardroom, or launching themselves onto the six o'clock news with their final speech to parliament, which turns out to contain a knockout punch for the prime minister, calxluxophiliacs love their moment in the sun.

[calx, lime; lux, light]

§

Chaophilia: delight in buying children noisy presents.

A typical chaophiliac is around 50-something, tanned and smug. They are often empty nesters who spent the first 20 years of their children's lives resenting the fact that their younger friends (often younger siblings) visited them with tales of nights enjoyed getting on down, living it up, and generally tripping the light fantastic. Now, it's payback time. Especially where younger siblings are concerned: figures show this is more common among aunts and uncles than it is, say, among grandparents, who do so much of the child-minding of their grandkids that noisy presents can backfire. Their enjoyment of gifting impossibly annoying toys is something they do little to mask. The latest *Doctor Who* 'head', which can be heard into the night, striking up its deletion mantra from the toy room. Or the musical gift, always a favourite. (Anyone who has ever been present to hear the line, 'A drum kit, wow, thanks Uncle Pete!' will be able to understand this.) A separate, occasionally more vindictive strain is *Chaophilia physica*, wherein the sufferer enjoys donating gifts that require the parents to engage in sporting activity of some sort. At its mildest, it is merely the gift of a football but more extreme cases have been known. ('Dad, Auntie Sue got me some boxing lessons. They're for you too!')

[chaos, chaos; physica, physical]

§

Cibsputophilia: delight in serving food that has been tampered with.

A specialised but nevertheless very common philia, allegedly rife within the catering community. The genuine cibsputophiliac is one who desires to do no damage via their actions. They merely seek some level of counterbalance, a degree of equalisation for the deemed shortcomings of the party at table four. Accordingly, the scale of post-preparation (food rearrangement, some call it) varies. Ordering while treating the waiter as if they are 'below stairs' might lead to the odd extra ingredient being added to your food, for example: a toe nail, cigarette butt or Band-Aid. Lesser crimes, such as returning to an eatery where one previously tipped badly, might simply gain you some invisible additions to the bill, leaving your food untouched. Worst among the perceived infractions is sending back food, which is said to carry an automatic sentence (or should I say garnish) of body fluids. We should probably leave this here and move on.

[cibus, food; sputum, spit]

᭄

Citubophilia: delight in throwing away good food.

A truly dark delight in this, or indeed any age, but one that has somehow managed to stay on the menu. A citubophiliac can usually trace their habit back to a time of food deprivation. In the case of the British, it stems from the food rationing of the second world war, which continued into the early 1950s. A dubious way of displaying both your status and taste was by what you were prepared to throw away. A citubophiliac is best typified by the character played by Maggie Smith in *A Private Function*, who relishes the moment she can donate some of her most needed rations to the slops destined to fatten a pig. Today, a version of this philia is still more prevalent than one might imagine, sometimes finding its outlet not just in the delight in wasting food but also water and light. The higher the establishment where one can practise one's *Citubophilia*, the greater the pleasure and, therefore, discomfort of others. Seeing a truffle ignored at the Wolseley, for example, is the equivalent of seven shocking courses at a Pizza Express. Delightful.

[cibus, food; tuber, dump]

§

Coclearophilia: delight in turning over to signal a lack of sex.

Many a coclearophile has enjoyed a small chuckle at the irony of this name, if informed by their friendly neighbourhood shrink – *cocleare* being the Latin word for spoon. Ah, one of their favourite positions. But, as Napoleon almost certainly never said, not tonight, Josephine. It is not necessarily that they do *not* want sex. Many more things than their own personal desires come into play which influence them into performing the famous 'Good Queen Bess' manoeuvre (the turnover through 180 degrees, with accompanying 'Night, night!', named after probably this country's most famous virgin). They might possibly be teaching their partner a lesson. They might be settling an argument. Indeed, even when the object of their Good Queen Bess perceives there to *be* no argument, they may still be settling an old argument: how old, only time or plenty of drink may tell. They might even be putting in some groundwork, an advance play, in order to make a future move (the less famous 'Randy King Richard' who reportedly had more conquests than his subjects had hot dinners) all the more surprising.

[cocleare, spoon]

Ϩ

Cogecolloquophilia: delight in witnessing someone forced into conversation on a train.

This is a beauty, and one of those things that tempt the author to think, from time to time, that there truly is a god. Chief among its pleasures is the fact that the person indulging themselves has to do precisely nothing: they are a lucky bystander who just happens to be in the right place at the right time. The work, in this philia, is all done by the victim and their tormentor. The most intense and therefore enjoyable strain is *Cogecolloquophilia commuta* in which the victim is a regular on the train, thus making for maximum embarrassment. The protagonist is very often an elderly person or a Christian – that is, someone who lives life as if it were 1950 and therefore is under the mistaken impression that people still talk on trains. The cogecolloquophiliac themselves, apparently deep in a book, headphones or laptop, will often be a nodding acquaintance of the victim, thus increasing the ecstasy. Of course, the book, headphones and laptop are all props: for they are actually enjoying the suitably loud conversation ensuing, often for the length of the entire journey, the perpetrator utterly unaware of her victim's pain. 'Oh, I see, young man, you are a CEO for GlaxoSmithKline... how lovely. And tell me do you have anything to do with that Viagra I've heard so much about? My son-in-law swears by it!' For maximum pleasure, the cogecolloquophiliac might offer to give up his double seat, making out that he presumes the two are together. Cruel but beautiful.

[cogere, to compel; colloquium, talk]

Comsecrophilia: delight in revealing the groom's bad habits in a speech.

Before 'The Downturn', weddings were building up a head of steam which meant that few mortals could afford to be invited to them. Local church halls had long since been replaced by plush hotels and then fairy castles. Stag dos had mushroomed from the drink down the pub ('Such a shame that Reddo wouldn't take a gap year for your stag, bad form!'). Accordingly, the best man's speech developed too. Previously, what might have been scribbled on the white side of the paper inside a pack of Rothmans grew into a sketch with props, then an act, with photos or video footage, before finally burgeoning into a Busby Berkeley routine, sung at the piano, while a troupe of dancing girls perform a choreographed routine. But then, as I say, came…The Downturn.

At the heart of it all, both pre- and post- 'The *', is a comsecrophile. His delight is not, as you might think, in the power of his position. It is in the *truth* of his position. He is desperate to tell you all he knows about this 'so-called all-round nice guy' they call the groom. He's kept it in for years. But no longer. Here he goes. With props. And video. And a line up of dancing girls, each one of whom, it turns out, the groom is less than pleased to see again. 'Ok, where shall I start on the subject of the groom. Let's begin… with his first kiss. Well, I say *kiss*…'.

* insert current buzz phrase. It used to be 'the Collapse', then 'the Slump', followed by 'the Depression'.

[communitas, public: secretus, secret]

§

Consocophilia: delight in printing a non-story in order to taunt those in possession of an injunction.

In my local, if the last orders bell ever did sound, it was usually around 15 minutes before we were unceremoniously asked to leave. (As an old friend used to always add, five minutes later and you get the sprinklers turned on: another five, they release the Dobermans.) For some reason, it took a little longer for the gentlemen of the press, drinking at the last chance saloon.

Consocophiliacs are, oddly enough, often to be found among the ranks of newspaper editors and deputy editors and they adore the practice of story-butting: placing one story beside another, the two seemingly unconnected but for the canny reader, very telling indeed, for the sheer delight in taunting the individual concerned. So one story might be headlined 'Philandering Pet-beating Lothario Gags Papers', while, immediately next door is the beaming face of an 'unrelated celebrity': 'Family Man X, pictured opening a supermarket. Er, last year'. A slightly macabre pleasure, made somewhat obsolete by the advent of Twitter.

[consociare, to associate]

§

Consorsophilia: delight in enforcing work power to the letter of the law.

It is highly likely that we have all dealt with consorsophiliacs at some point in our lives. At work, while they were either under us, or on the same level, they were, I think it's fair to say, our friends. We called them friends, we went for drinks after work, we went to lunch. All was well. Then, they received their promotion making them, strictly speaking, above us. In work terms. Now, they call us 'colleagues', they don't go for drinks, and if they do lunch – quite rare – they insist on paying 'because you can't afford it' and they make a point of telling us they can put it on expenses. It is more than likely that these people, apart from being complete pains in the seat region, are now consorsophiliacs. They probably gain their delights from enforcing their power at work. And to the letter. 'Can you get onto ordering the paper clips for the north-east region, please? And don't forget the regional colour coordination. Bristol are using green glossy when they should be matt black.' 'Absolutely', you reply, 'I'm onto it. Should have it done by tomorrow'. They smile. 'No, we need it by 9 p.m. tonight, because the Sunderland office are on a late one and will process it *as soon as*. And while you're at it, can you guestimate the Tippex situation.' You laugh. As your titter peters out, you look at the CEO for Former Friendships. He *is* smiling. But a weird kind of smile. It's a smile that says: I love my power. And his arched eyebrows are adding: And I don't have lots so I'm making sure I enjoy what I've got! You know the worst thing about this situation? With an attitude like *that*, in a workplace like *yours*… he's bound to go far.

[consors, workfriend]

Contramophila: delight in
pricking a love bubble.

The person who groans towards the end of *Four Weddings And a Funeral*, when Andy MacDowell says, in the middle of a veritable monsoon: 'Is it raining? I hadn't noticed', is not necessarily a contramophiliac. No. Think of the phrase 'hopeless romantics'. Got them in your head? Now think of the absolute opposite. They are often easier to pitch than their diametrically opposing counterparts. No-nonsense, practical and often with a scientific bent, they treat 'romance' in much the same way as Richard Dawkins treats religion: a series of unfounded non-sequiturs which needs correcting. So they do, and they enjoy the process, often to the detriment of those around them. We need not concern ourselves too long with such types, whose environment is its own reward. Their delights come from a multitude of tiny actions: refusing to give up their place in a double seat on a train for a couple despite being asked; seeing children as just smaller people and in no way fluffy or cute; and preferring obscure film seasons from Chile to Richard Curtis movies. These poor people!

[contra, against; amo, love]

§

Creverophilia: delight in believing one is right.

See *Indiverophilia*.

[credo, believe; vero, truth]

§

Currophilia: delight in the small, unnecessary journey by car.

Currophiliacs are the mechanical equivalent of smokers in public. If they could afford to buy a personalised number plate that read UPY0 UR5, they would. They simply adore the small, unnecessary journey by car. They have long since given up trying to explain 'Sorry,

I left it *so* last minute, I had to run up here in the car!'
Now, they simply smile and drive on. They love their car
like a baron loves his smelly, feudal subject – it's theirs
and they'll abuse it if they want to. In their car, all makes
sense. They press a button, and something happens.
They put their foot down, and everything changes. It is
their world. Usually, they are by no means flat-earthers
either, when it comes to green issues. They switch off
their lights at home, they separate their bins, they even
occasionally watch *Countryfile*. However, they simply
love their little car. It is, after all, their black delight.

[currus, chariot]

ॐ

Denegarophilia: delight in a friend's card being refused.

'Oh, I felt so embarrassed for him'. No you didn't.
'I didn't know where to look.' You were looking
straight into his eyes, smiling. You even dribbled a
little without realising. 'He said it must be some sort of
mistake, there was plenty of money in that account.'
Yeah, right! At last, you've been proven correct – the
guy's a fraud, a sad, broke fraud who clearly hasn't
got two *sous* to rub together and only invited you
out so that you could pay up when he tried his old
'Declined? Really, are you sure?' trick on you.

Ok, it's not always as virulent as that. Sometimes a
denegarophile doesn't even know the person being
declined. They might be in the next lane at the
supermarket checkout. But once it has been refused,

the denegarophile feels a little extra warmth inside for the length of time it takes to size the offending cardholder up. Mmm, well, look at them. Hardly surprising, really. See also *Vinoptophilia*.

[denegaro, refuse]

ട്

Dissemmophilia: delight in having someone on speakerphone without their knowledge.

One of the more minor office pleasures, certainly less pleasurable than *Aldarophilia* (qv) but perhaps a little higher on the scale than stealing a single toilet roll from the loos to tide you over until the supermarket home delivery van comes. If you are part of a workforce, one of what Stalin jokingly called 'the great unwatched'* then you pass the achingly laborious time at the office by experiencing a series of tiny, sometimes almost microscopic, gains in your head. They might be gains at the expense of your employers or gains at the expense of your colleagues. Dissemophiles fall into this latter category. For them, putting you on speakerphone is up there with having avoided their turn in the tea rota and is less likely to be any outward manifest of a personal vendetta than a sad tick in the timesheet of their careers that will see them retiring early at 55 with a small whip round and an impersonal speech. Of course, the full definition of *Dissemmophilia* should include the line 'without your knowledge' for this is where their pleasure lies – the usually vain hope that you will say something embarrassingly inappropriate (bronze), truly humiliating (silver) or career endangering (gold).

* *All Work and No Pay* by Keith Stalin (*MCPS and bar*), YouPub Press

[disseminare, to broadcast]

ဖ

Diuophilia: delight in taking hours to get ready.

I once visited a recording studio which specialised in the production of adverts. While being taken through the space-age sound desk in front of me, I ventured to ask the purpose of one particularly prominent button, in red, which had its own special area. 'Oh, that. That's the Client Button'. It turned out this was a button that troublesome, talentless clients – those who would not know good production if it came and bit them in the ears – could turn to their heart's content to bring up or turn down a certain effect. The button in question didn't actually do anything tangible at all and literally was not connected to the rest of the desk. However, each time a take was made, the producers would look at the client and say 'Are you happy with that mix?' and the client would say 'Hang on…' And adjust his little button. 'There. That's a little better.' With everyone happy, progress could be made.

It is said that many female diuophiliacs (it is mainly a female philia) have an endless supply of 'client button' equivalents in their handbags and their bedrooms: a limitless supply of powders and paints, lotions and creams, each designed to do absolutely nothing tangible at all, save to add to the process where a wife or partner suspends time prior to an urgent appointment. To be fair, very few women will be aware of this philia – only a tiny number will admit to it, usually after a particularly irksome domestic. The majority go through life in denial, simply enjoying the pleasure of being '… *nearly ready!*'

[diu, long time]

§

Duodomophilia: delight in having a second home.

The delight in having a second home lies not in the visiting thereof but in dropping it into conversation. A great deal of pleasure might be derived from a question fielded about the picture on the lavatory wall with a rather nice villa in the background (indeed, the same one that features in a jolly large number of the pictures round the house). Virtual paroxysms of quasi-orgasmic delight, however, are attained via those conversations where the owner doesn't even have to point out the dual nature of his home-owning status, but has it drawn out of them by a seemingly interested party. It is the equivalent of receiving a compliment about a truly expensive outfit and replying 'Oh, what, *this* old thing?' A pure delight, bettered only if the practitioner finds themselves pestered with heavy-handed hints at, or overt requests for, holidays. Then, the joys are raised to another level, as if the duodomophile is holding a candle flame inside a window, watching an unsuspecting poor moth batter his head vainly against it.

[duo, two; domus, home]

Eboracophilia: delight in plain speaking.

It is widely reported that when Julius Caesar was assassinated, he cried out '*Et tu, Brute!*' to his one-time friend, Marcus Brutus, who was leading the assault. What is less well known is the retort from his erstwhile companion, namely '*Scio quae placet et quae amo scio!*' Over the years, this has led many a scholar to the conclusion that, as well as Cyprus and Crete, Brutus must, at some point, have taken in Yorkshire on his travels.

Eboracophiliacs love using their language like a dagger to puncture what they see as the waffle of others. Often taking an almost geographical delight in their bluntness, they adore their own concise phrasing, surprising even themselves with just how many situations are best dealt with by the simple utterance of the word 'Bollocks!' Always best talked out of a career in the diplomatic service (nor are they totally suited to drafting legal documents), their favourite pastimes are posh-person baiting (see *Benedixophilia*) or watching re-runs of *McCloud.*

[Scio quae placet et quae amo scio, I know what I like and I like what I know; Eboracum, York]

Extrunophilia: delight in sailing past a queue because you're on the guest list.

Extrunophiles are simply logical people. Who would not want to be on the guest list? Think about it: a guest is welcome, a guest is wanted, a guest *doesn't pay*. This isn't a *lodger* list, it's a guest list. Who, in their right mind, wouldn't want to be on a guest list? The extrunophile knows this, in their head. They treat the queue for … (insert latest 'it' club here*) as a red carpet and their dance – for it is a dance, and not a walk – past the queue and up to the front is practised and perfected to be just right. The lack of eye-contact with the crowd; the clear demonstration of dominance over their partner (lest you, heaven forbid, think *they* might be the 'plus one'); the nod to the bouncer, complete with first name exchange. All these things are the 'desiderata' of the long-term extrunophile. Occasionally, serendipity might add a further frisson and allow them to take a call on their mobile while they are mid-dance. 'Hey, Leonardo, man!' they shout into their phones, as they sail through the door (leaving Grandma, who called to ask for help with the Sky Plus, totally bemused). To categorize this 'delight', it is necessary to understand the joys experienced by the sufferer. They delight in the fact that they clearly haven't paid.

Again, as so many times before, this is not a monetary issue: simply one of privilege. An extrunophile would no more pay for entry than the Queen would carry money. They love the feeling of being valued by their hosts. They take pleasure in sensing that you might well be thinking 'Ooh, are they famous: should I know them?' in much the same, feeble-minded way that a man standing in the street looking upwards but at nothing in particular might eventually gather a crowd around him, also looking upward. At nothing in particular. Worthy of separate mention are *Extrunophilia oves* sufferers. These sorry individuals delight in gaining access to the roped off VIP sections of the same establishments, where they can jostle for far too little space with minor league football players, former reality TV contestants and a girl who once read the weather on Meridian.

*This name changed eight times from writing up to going to print so has now been left vacant for you to fill in. In pencil.

[Extra, plus; unum, one; oves, sheep]

§

Falsomnophilia: delight in pretending to be asleep.

Despite most people thinking this might have been initially a childhood delight, the pleasures of *Falsomnophilia* are almost entirely enjoyed in later years, particularly *Falsomnophilia virgina*. First the four strains: *secretia*, *labria*, *magisomnia* and the aforementioned *virgina*. *Falsomnophilia secretia* involves feigning sleep in order to eavesdrop. Generally, occasions present themselves almost by chance, so any eavesdropping must be done on a general 'fishing' basis, to see what one might catch.

Sometimes fruits are good, particularly on joint holidays where two families share the same villa. *Falsomnophilia laboria* is employed, often by males, to get themselves out of jobs, particularly those involving assembling flatpack furniture. Who among us has not heard a classic *laboria* conversation on the lines of:

'Aw, look he's fallen asleep, poor love.'

'Poor love? He's a lump, and he's got to grout the bathroom!'

'He's tired out.'

'He's a git.'

Falsomnophilia magisomnia is possibly the simplest and earliest form, feigned in order to extend the possibility of sleep, i.e., the classic lie-in. This is what the majority enjoy on Sunday mornings or during student term time. Finally, there is the most useful and, some say, most enjoyable: *Falsomnophilia virgina*. Here, practitioners fake their sleep to prevent sexual contact.

[falsus, fake; somnus, sleep; virginis, virgin; secretus, secret; laboro, work; magis somno, more sleep]

Famaphilia: delight in being famous.

This is the root condition that leads to all the others: *Mefamaphilia*, *Tefamaphilia*, even *Nomecrophilia* (qv all). This is the crock of gold at the end of the rainbow for the last few generations, who spent their later teenage years looking for the golden ticket at the Job Centre which read 'Wanted: Person to be Famous. No qualifications necessary'. Eventually, one or two made it, either via sleeping with a stranger on *Samoan Big Brother 19* or by eating so much that a documentary crew turned up at their home to film their removal by crane. To call this a delight is, literally, true. Famaphiliacs – genuine ones – do love their fame and love the fact that their family or their friends may not have it. Indeed, they enjoy those supplementary pleasures of pointing out to their sister that she is always labelled 'Sister of…' by the paparazzi press, rather than by her own name. Ultimately, though, it is a hollow pleasure, one much like playing rugby or dogging: it's often fun during the rough and tumble, but only leaves them feeling dirty afterwards.

[fama, fame]

ᵹ

Ferinfanophilia: delight in witnessing the tantrums of someone else's child

Not quite an aviphile nor vidicophile (both qv), the ferinfanophile enjoys a more subtle pleasure. Usually, there is nothing to tell them apart from mere mortals other than the tiniest flicker of a smile, so gentle that you are unsure it's there, which appears on their face when they are in sight of another person's child having a tantrum. Besides, you are more than a little side-tracked by your two-year-old whirling dervish mutating into a Brother of Satan in the local cafe to be able to identify them. If a ferinfanophiliac feels like they have not truly made their point, they may resort to a hint of *Infrenophilia* (qv). A classic ferinfanophiliac question always begins with the words 'Is that *your* little darling who is…'. Then comes the delicious detail: '…pulling the wallpaper off the state room wall?'; '…being carried over there, kicking and screaming, by the *maître d'*?'; and my personal favourite '…sitting in the middle of Centre Court? I don't think you're encouraged to do *that* to the grass, are you?'

[ferus, wild; infans, child]

§

Findophilia: delight in 'copying in' superiors on relevant emails.

This surely counts as one of the greatest of the modern philias. The findophiliac derives pleasure from dropping their colleague from a great height into a whole wave of cybercrap by copying in their superiors to emails that their colleagues would rather their boss never saw. The closer that person sits to them in the office environment, the greater the pleasure. It would be a findophilac's dream to copy superiors in on a message that would actually have arrived later by email than if they could have delivered it in person. Very often the ideal situation for a sufferer would involve the planted question (see *Infrenophilia*) but not always. Sometimes, they might simply be fishing for any potential mischief which might happen to be out there. Blind copying is of no interest to the findophile who needs to know that the damage will be done: any chance that the recipient might not know about it and, well, where's the *Schadenfreude* in that? Invariably, the damage *is* done, though. On rare occasions, it can backfire if the subject matter either a) goes back and forwards too much or b) is too trivial. There is little pleasure to be gleaned from copying in the chairman and chief executive on 'the kid's bedroom mess that is the photocopying room'.

[findo, split]

§

Flagrophilia: delight in burning things in your garden.

Let me make myself clear: one must not think of pyromania or arson when thinking about *Flagrophilia*. For the flagrophiliac, the pleasure is not in the burning, it is in the effects of the burning. For a standard sufferer, if the home is the castle, then the back garden is the personal fiefdom. Here, according to the unwritten bill of rights, it is their personal birthright, nay duty, to play loud music, sunbathe in the nude and slap their own children across the back of the legs for telling lies. The bill extends beyond these divine pleasures, though, and, somewhere along the way, takes in 'Thou shalt openly burn the waste of thy rear garden – with license extending to the front, also – on a day most visible to thine neighbours. And, yea, thou shouldst employ a brazier.' (It is fair to say that, other than criminals who want to foolishly dispose of evidence in order to look particularly suspicious to our favourite TV detective, the chief users of braziers are flagrophiliacs.) Even though the price of landfill is not really an issue to the flagrophiliac, neither do they love 'the burn', so to speak. They love the *smoke*. Indeed, their motto, 'There's No Fire Without Smoke' pretty well says as much. In terms of spotting them, well, this is not too hard: simply follow the plume of smoke. To find *Flagrophilia maxima* sufferers, follow the plume of smoke... back to your washing line.

Many sufferers are known to get excited watching old cowboy movies. The bits where the Indians make smoke signals.

[flagrantia, burning]

ʒ

Flavophilia: delight in blocking someone's exit.

At first glance, this might appear a mix of aggression and obstinacy but the key is in the full name. This is 'delight in blocking another vehicle's exit from a box junction even though you can't move yourself'. As such, this is no rare rapture. Indeed it is a weekly if not daily delight. Naturally, for such a common philia, there are a diverse range of sub-strains. *Flavophilia praeter* is the most prevalent. Sufferers choose to enjoy themselves as if in a freeze frame photo: they maintain their gaze firmly forwards, two hands on the wheel at ten to two, and merely imagine the motorist currently having a blue fit to their right. *Flavophilia risa* is one stage on in both bravery and, so I'm told, pleasure rating. These hardy individuals enjoy their 'box time' (as Apple might have called it had they invented it) by slowly rotating their faces to the screaming banshee they have blocked and simply smiling. Full on Queen's Gallantry medals should be awarded to those foolhardy individuals who enjoy *Flavophilia superba*. These Mad Maxes are fierce in their triumphant glee. They relish their position, they face off, they remonstrate. They are hospitalised, on occasion, too. Incidentally, it should be noted that there are allegedly some groups – hippies, nuns, born-again Christians, etc – who think that the number of times you let someone in (or out, or through, in fact) precisely corresponds to the number of times you, yourself, are let in (out, through). These people are clearly not great mathematicians.

[flavus, yellow; praetermittere, ignore; risus, smile; superbus, proud]

ﬥ

Foedulavophilia: delight in
raising private material in public.

The first forms of *Foedulavophilia* were recorded on the walls of the forum in ancient Rome and came in the form of graffiti. Lines such as 'Hic Kilroi erat' and the follow-up line, 'casu, ipse signum suum fundum', are still preserved today for the benefit of tourists and scholars alike. As with so many of the delights in this book, it operates on different levels for different disciples. *Foedulavophilia ignosca* is the vanilla flavour, whose currency is light information which mildly embarrasses its victims. The sufferer is often able to maintain a close relationship with their subject, despite the seemingly random broadcast of level one material. For example, many are spouses, passing on work gossip at dinner parties, or friends introducing details of embarrassing school anecdotes and minor gaffes of old. Into this enjoyable, some might say fun, category some lesser medical ailments might be introduced – Athlete's foot, for example.

Foedulavophilia non ignosca is an entirely different animal and not to be indulged in lightly. It takes a master to pleasure themselves at this level and still maintain friendship status. At this level, major medical details are dropped into conversations with Molotovian abandon, often by erupting mothers-in-law who have lain dormant for years, lulling their prey into thinking they did in fact think he *was* good enough for their daughter. Spouses, at this level, are dealing in major work plans, unknown to the invited colleagues round the table and occasionally leading to hasty mobile phone conversations from hallways. Early carriages, even. Very often, this is the delight of a spouse, enjoyed in return for a perceived dressing room slight or an inadequate sexual performance. 'Oh my, don't tell me you didn't know about that? Darling, I thought you told me Chris and his team had already had their P45s? Oh, Chris, I'm so sorry. More syllabub?

One wonderfully nuanced version of *Foedulavophilia* exists which doctors find very hard to accurately diagnose, and this is *Foedulavophilia infans*. This refers to the disclosed facts revealed by children in apparent innocence, sometimes in public, sometimes at home but usually in school, to a teacher. A potentially roginfanophiliac (qv) teacher, perhaps. 'Do we have to have water, Mrs Griffin? My mummy says vodka has exactly the same taste. She and my daddy drink lots. Mummy said: "It helps me get through awful rumpy-pumpy with your father". Miss, what's rumpy-pumpy?' Doctors are divided: a child's inadvertent mistake? Or revenge for early bedtimes and healthy food?

[foedus, dirty; lavationem, washing; casu, ipse signum suum fundum, by the way, he has a boil on his bum; ignosco, forgive]

Fortanotophilia: delight in leading someone on.

If it comes as a shock that there is a largely female version of *Nonexilophilia* (qv), then perhaps you are the sort of person who married their childhood sweetheart, didn't have sex beforehand and then lived like Rock Hudson and Doris Day with time off only to write home to mum. The fortanotophile builds up a fake wall, brick by brick, of a hint of a soupçon of an impression that there is a chance. And then, to a fixed timescale, they destroy the wall in one swoop. If their turf is the workplace, then the fortanotophiliac must be careful to select their victims from among those who have no hand on the tiller of power: when the fortanotophile bubble bursts, things can get bleak. Usually, fortanotophiliacs operate an unwritten league system in all things, whether wittingly or not: brands, countries, film stars and, of course, people themselves are all in unspoken leagues. When it comes to people, statistically speaking, most fortanotophiles tend to put themselves in a high league, and their victims in a far lower one.

[fortasse, maybe; non, not]

ꚉ

Forvoxophilia: delight in speaking loudly.

Frankly, whatever we might say to the contrary, who doesn't love the sound of their own voice – very loud – at certain times? This perennial favourite is present in all of us from childhood times, when it is used principally to tell on siblings and smelly school friends. In adulthood, it is enjoyed in a number of different ways. There is the strain *Forvoxophilia informationa*, used to pass on information in an overly conspicuous way, for the purpose of giving hints. For example, the following line while guests are present: 'Shall I go into the kitchen now and START TO MAKE THE DINNER, Ken?' [translation: Stop flirting with that woman who's young enough to be your daughter and help me make the dinner, KEN!]

Overdoing one's pleasure here can result in discomfort for guests or even giving the unintentional impression that one is somehow caught up in a hostage scenario and, like Lassie, is trying to tell us something. Chances are Lassie had a quieter bark. Overall, the most common strain of *Forvoxophilia* is used by spouses to embarrass partners, usually wives to husbands. Examples abound, providing everyday joy for millions, through inexplicably loud emphasis of information – information perfect for humiliation. 'George, are you sure you should be dancing with your secretary... with YOUR HERNIA?'

There is a type of *Forvoxophilia* for hangover situations although this is a totally separate disorder, dealt with under *Noconcordophilia* (qv).

[fortis, loud; vox, voice; information, information]

§

Fracurrophilia: delight in passing a broken-down Ferrari in your clapped out Micra (or sim.).

It should be pointed out that this definition might seem a little limited. The 'or sim.' is important, then. It translates as literally 'delight in the broken chariot', rather than the specifically branded version used above. Nevertheless, whether it be Messala smiling fiendishly as his knife wheels razor into Ben Hur's or, as is more common, a friendly look which pretends to say 'You OK?' as your dull, small car passes the Boxter laid out on the hard shoulder, the feelings are one and the same. Perfecting the 'You OK?' look is everything to the fracurrophiliac. It should include the mouthed words themselves, a part worried, part Wallace (of Wallace and Gromit) smile and a hint of crikey. But only a hint. The blend should produce a look which says to the driver of the broken down car 'I'm not going to stop, you know. Not in a million years!' Only when the sufferer is past the said car can he look in his wing mirror.

And smile.

A full, long Wallace.

[currus, chariot; fractus, broken]

§

Furlinuophilia: delight in issuing your 'full and unqualified support'.

To be entirely accurate, the definition above of this particular philia is both partial and qualified. A more precise one might read 'delight in issuing your full and unqualified support for a colleague, almost always in the theatre of politics, and almost always as a time-buying exercise and therefore prior to the unceremonious and opportune dumping of the said colleague so that they might spend more time with their family'. That said, it is hopefully an unwittingly sad political animal that delights in this sort of stuff, perhaps even one which tells themselves that they are doing things for the greater political good. And then tells everyone their favourite knock-knock joke (it's the one that goes: 'Knock Knock.' 'Who's there?' '[Insert sacked person's name here]'. '[Insert sacked person's name here] who?' 'Ah, how soon we forget.') A truly insidious delight.

[furca, fork: lingua, tongue]

§

Fustisophilia: delight in being thin.

Accurate numbers of how many fustisophiles are actually out there do not exist. This is partially due to a lack of funding for many *Schadenfreude*-related activities – a distressing situation, in this author's view – but mainly because, at present, model Kate Moss has been the only one pioneering enough to openly admit to her fondness for all things slim. 'Nothing tastes as good as skinny feels' has become the motto for a movement which has had to continue to exist unseen, due in no little part to the fact that its followers are standing sideways. In this age of health and wealth, *Fustisophilia* is genuinely the philia that dare not speak its name. It is hidden by its practitioners for whom the idea of five-a-day is used more as an exact measure than a concept: five leaves of lettuce, for example, or, if they are having a day off, five slices of apple.

A fustisophile is not, it should be stressed, an anorexic, although there is a certain level of eating disorderliness at play. A fustisophile opts in and out of their beliefs, much as a casual Catholic might tick the boxes of their preference as if completing a doorstep survey: yes to the Jesus bit; no to the transubstantiation, if you don't mind; oh, and a definite no to the birth control nonsense, thank you very much. So a fustisophile only indulges sporadically. When they do, however, they love every moment, patting themselves side-on in the mirror or retrieving those next-size-down jeans with a whoop of dark delight, forgetting the tortuous path, studded with sacrifice, that led them there. Related but different is *Uncidamnophilia*, in which each reclaimed hole in the slimmer's belt is greeted with sheer delight and a celebration involving junk food.

[fustis, stick; uncia, inch; damnum, loss]

Hodiephilia: delight in asking a politician a tough question.

It became accepted wisdom, in the late 20th and early 21st centuries, that the political interview should be 'on subject'; that a politician should be granted both the freedom and the airtime to wax lyrical on a single subject at will, thus allowing them to purge themselves of their well-rehearsed soundbites. Thankfully, hodiephiliacs have put an end to all this, delighting in almost guerilla questioning on any subject they so please. So, an unsuspecting advocate invited to be interviewed on the pros and cons of fluffiness in family pets might instead find themselves being asked about terrorist rendition. Or the personal sexual peccadilloes of an incumbent PM. Below the belt, perhaps, in another age, but nowadays almost a spectator sport.

[hodie, today]

§

Immotophilia: delight in having a seat on the train, while those around you stand.

One of few almost entirely mute philias, partly due to the nature of the fields on which immotophiliacs do battle. Interestingly, there are no identifying catchphrases which would make spotting an immotophiliac a little easier. *Immotophilia* is most common in seasoned (for which read cynical) commuters usually travelling on fast, overland trains (for trains read boiling pots of tormented souls). These hardened types long ago learnt the joys of precision morning drills, mindless clustering around train doors and, of course, the almost exquisite joy of silence.* Once en route, either in silence or oblivious MP3-dom, it is then that unlucky latecomers – or, even worse, the poor unfortunates joining the train later down the line, seen very much as the poor cousins of the commuter world – will witness the immotophile in action. In an increasingly sardine-like environment, and not to be mistaken for pertinophiles (qv), they will delight in using their full personal space, despite the crush: this might mean utilising a stilt-walker's quota of leg room or wildly opening and closing their newspaper as if measuring up the potential for swinging cats. They relish their trademark 'tut' when a fellow passenger dares to move their elbows a hair's breadth to avoid another bout of cramp. Long term immotophiliacs will deliberately refuse to look up when one more elderly, one more pregnant or even one more disabled person pops into their peripheral vision. More chronic sufferers will have developed the more acquired taste – akin to the olive in the suburban travel world – of looking up, and smiling sweetly at the aging unfortunate before burying their head back in *Management Today*.

* Some immotophiliacs will break the code of silence if they have either wittingly or inadvertently become members of a club, a band of disparate folk brought together by nothing more than a frosty nod and a shared journey plan. These are not ambitious expedition clubs but merely routine journey cliques, often uniting people from uniquely differing backgrounds: they may never cross datelines, but they occasionally cross payscales.

[immotus, not moving]

ક

Imverbophilia: delight in using jargon.

At one stage, in the late 1970s, it was hoped that *Imverbophilia* would be able to be contained among the pioneering workers who did so much to promote it, namely teachers. Cue the faintly ridiculous 1980s and the arrival of the so-called yuppie and it was soon clear this was going to be a delight that spread to all walks of life. *Imverbophilia* is, essentially, a misnomer as it began its life as a delight in acronyms – hence the rash of practitioners in the teaching world. Teachers do still make up a huge percentage of this strange bunch, feigning a healthy scepticism of 'wankwords' and 'acrony-ism' while at the same time launching as many WYSIWYGs,[*] MBWAs[**] and TSAs[***] per second as they can. Local councils are said to be one of the prime breeding grounds for imverbophiliacs. Indeed, one former government insider, in a soon-to-be-published memoir, alleges that the real idea behind The Big Society came to David Cameron when he was sent a parking notice and couldn't understand a word of the form.[****]

[*] What you see is what you get
[**] Management by walking about
[***] Totally Spurious Acronym
[****] *Total Bullingdon* by Robin Porr, pre-pub.copy marked 'Do Not Quote, for NOTW serialisation only'.

[impars, odd; verbum, word]

§

Inacanvophilia: delight in over-branding one's clothes.

Don't let the etymology of this delight fool you. The 'blank canvas' has long gone. It was the root of the inacanvophile's problem in the first place, only to be replaced by their all-encompassing search for brand fulfilment. An inacanvophile feels validated by brands and enjoys putting as many of them about their person as possible. At one point, it was the premium brand that was king, now it is simply 'any brand will do' as every available item of clothing shouts a name – so that the bearer doesn't have to. Where there might once have been Gucci and D&G,

now any sense of discernment is gone: Tesco Shirt, Hovis shorts, Armitage Shanks socks – the brand name is *not* the issue, so long as it *is* a brand. The dark joy element comes into play in more youthful settings, where the peer-pressured pool that is the teenage years means that one man's over-brand can be another man's feeling of inadequacy. If only the wearer would realise that the brand ecosystem could be reversed overnight with just a little game of 'hard to get'. Until then, or the moment they start to sell tattoo rights, the only blank space left is in their brains.

[inanus, blank; canvas, canvas]

Inauctophilia: delight in anonymity.

One of the more subtle delicacies in this book, *Inauctophilia* is often not even *tangibly* enjoyed, even by inauctophiles. For this is not the delights of being 'famous but unrecognised' – a feat increasingly hard to pull off in a world where even the postman delivering your copies of *My Big Fat Gweek Wedding – A West Country Special*, has 100,000 followers on Twitter. *Inauctophilia* is the delight in relative anonymity – that is a love of not being the person you are because of geographical or situational displacement. So, a parent, away on business, will delight in eating alone, or sitting in a crowded wine bar, taking in all around them. If this sounds a lot like snooping then that would be right: a great many facets of *Inauctophilia* and snooping are shared. Where the pleasure is at its most heavenly, though, and veering on to the darker side, is on the humble train journey. Here, reckless conversations still take place, with inauctophiles ready to enjoy the opportunity. The high-ranking TV industry insiders, chatting openly about share-sensitive future plans, while the high-ranking TV industry inauctophile sits by their side, their identity pleasingly unknown. Priceless.

[Incerti, uncertain; auctoris, source]

§

Incedophilia: delight in asking a sleeping person if they are asleep.

When is a question not a question? In this instance, when it is a badly concealed wake-up call with implicit amorous overtones. Or in some instances, explicit. Incedophiliacs are cynical masters at the shoulder-shake and 'polite' question 'Are you asleep?' in full knowledge that their subject is indeed exactly that. In many cases, this is followed up with a repeat of the same, to ensure effectiveness. Sometimes it has to be asked again and again before the person being questioned gives the *correct* answer. Occasionally, it might need to be followed by a heartfelt 'Oh, sorry, did I wake you?' The mild form, *Incedophilia prima*, strikes when one partner goes to bed first, while the other, who will be 'up soon', finds that the saucy bits in the remainder of the film, or possibly even inadvertent channel hopping, have left them 'up for it'. *Incedophilia secunda* is wholly more dark and occurs during the dead of night, when Glenn Miller Syndrome* has rendered one partner or other inexplicably 'in the mood'.

*So called because it not only leads to mood enhancement but also can act like GM himself. One moment, there's the amazing horn: next it's lost in mysterious circumstances.

[incedare, to stalk]

§

Incurrophilia: delight in witnessing a train passenger's mobile phone losing its signal.

There are no official statistics available for this assertion (oddly enough, no one has yet deemed this an area of research vital to human existence) but the author has used Pythagorean Laws of Probability, aka sheer guesswork, to posit that around 98 per cent of the population are incurrophiles. Admit it: the foghorn replacement on the phone, who is currently brandishing his company's profit and loss accounts and insisting they are broadcast to your whole carriage, is a complete derrière discomfort. The delicious moment when, despite the fact that the entire train could see the tunnel coming (indeed, some of them can tell you, to the second, when the tunnels will occur: sad but true) Mr Leghorn could not, results in an exquisite conversation. One that you are all too happy to hear. 'Yeah, and we should tell Tricia that if she doesn't buck her ideas up and get those numbers up to…hello? Hello? Keith?… Can you hear me?' If there were a YouTube channel for internal thoughts, the communal 'Thank goodness for that! Tosser!' which everyone on the train simultaneously thought would get a million hits. If the 1980s were the age of the train, according to Jimmy Saville, then perhaps, sadly, we are now in the age of the train tosser. Regardless, in these post-austerity times, it is perhaps good that someone can raise a communal smile on the way to work.

[currus, chariot]

§

Indicophilia: delight in asking for ID.

In a recent article for drinks industry magazine, *Optics*, Alana Koh-Pop established that more than 70 per cent of indicophiliacs are also solopusophiliacs (qv). This comes as no shock to those whose experience of the bar/nightclub working environment leads them to seek small pleasures wherever they can find them. As a result, relieving the tedium of the job by asking a grown man, in front of his rugby club friends, for his ID is fast becoming the norm. A more profound black delight can be gained from refusing port and lemons to people with zimmer frames who fail to produce their papers. Sometimes, of course, mistakes can be made. Asking a thirty-something female for ID, for example, can often produce the opposite effect and leave the object radiant for some days afterwards, thus draining the indicophile of all dark joy. Indeed, whether they realise it or not, the thirty-something females in question are, medically speaking at least, temporarily suffering from *Indicophilia inversa*. Sadly, it wears off.

[indicum, proof; inversus, inverse]

Indiverophilia: delight in being proven right

The whole area of what psycho-therapists term 'the *verophilias*' is a little bit of a minefield, but let's attempt to navigate it. First, there are indiverophiliacs. For these people, the moment of proof is in no way a punch-the-air 'Yes!' moment. They are simply – literally – delighted to have been somehow *proven* right and their delight in no way relates to winning over others. However, many indiverophiles have also, at some time, been verophiles. These are people who delight in simply *being* right. Statistically these people often end up working for Amnesty International, Greenpeace or the BBC. A related but again different area is *Creverophilia*, where the practitioner merely *believes* themselves to be right (see psychopaths, mass murderers, *Daily Mail* journalists, etc). For more in-depth reading on the whole subject, try '*The Plight of Right – You Can't go Wrong!*' by I. Emil, author. With regards to all of the above, it is not to be confused with *Rictusophilia* (qv).

[indicum, proof; vero, right; credere, to believe]

Infansophilia libera: delight in letting your own children go unchecked.

Never let an 'infansophilia librarian' – such a cool name – convince you that they are in any way pursuing their political beliefs. They do not let their children run wild because of any deeply-held belief in the essential freedom that children need to experience. Nor is it because they are essentially trying a different method of upbringing to you and 'Gina Ford is a thing of the past, man!' No, the plain truth is one of three things. One, they are children of the 1960s and they simply don't give a monkey's that little Lucien has just emptied all the wooden stirrers that Starbucks currently owns into your handbag. Two, and possibly worse, they are simply enjoying the only hour of free time they have had all week and, frankly, even if *The Observer* were to simply print out lines from the B&Q trade catalogue, it would still command their attention over anything their children were doing, no matter how vile or potentially illegal.

The final option, if proven to be the case, is much more worrying for the people around them. The third-case scenario is one in which you, the friends, are empty nesters and they, the infansophilia librarians, are your Torquemadas. They resent your total lack of dependents and your freedom to eat in public without any censuring opprobrium. So, they are opting out. They are unconcerned, nay over the moon, that their children are driving you bonkers, even if they are not using the time to read papers or catch up on sleep. Catchphrases include: 'Oh, he's only having fun!' And

'Aww, look. I think that means he likes you', as their three-year-old empties his barbecue sauce bucket onto your Blackberry.

[infans, children: libera, free]

§

Infrenophilia: to delight in asking a seemingly innocent question.

As its place in this book might suggest, this concerns a question to which one invariably knows the awful answer. Etymologically speaking, it stems from *infans renidens* (the words for laughing child), an all too apt derivation. In some areas of Northumberland, many still refer to this practice as 'to proffer the knobbly allsort', a curious phrase said to stem from the period when liquorice allsorts were the young child's confectionary of choice (as opposed to today when hard drugs are preferred). It was then common practice, once the favourite allsorts had been devoured from the 'quarter', to share round a bag containing only the allsorts you didn't like – invariably the round, knobbly, jelly-filled ones – happy in the knowledge that, although they appeared delightful, they were, in fact, odious.

Hence, to proffer the knobbly allsort is to offer up a seemingly innocent suggestion, or question, knowing full well that the answer will result in embarrassment or worse for the subject. It is most common in the work scenario, especially at higher levels. Here there exist only colleagues, not friends.

The apparently angelic voice saying 'Oh, Clive, how's the Hong Kong operation going?', knows only too well that the Hong Kong operation is screwed to the tune of more than $3 million and that it was indeed the unfortunate Clive who was hook, line and sinker responsible. The subject is an accomplished infrenophiliac – he is delighting in proffering the knobbly allsort. Socially, infrenophiliacs might ask 'So, did you get away anywhere nice this year?' when they know that the subject is financially challenged – downsizing even – and in place of Chamonix had to settle for a staycation, or even camping on the Humberside coast.

[infans, child: renidens, laughing]

§

Innatophilia: delight in a 'primary' talent. Just as there are primary colours, so there are primary talents. Within these primary talents, there are both *primary* primary talents and *secondary* primary talents. *Primary* primary talents are things which can be done with either just the bare hands or perhaps with the addition of the odd item left carelessly lying around: so, roofing, brickwork, and so on. Carpentry is probably chief among the *primary* primary talents, its position confirmed when Jesus Christ himself picked it out of the window at the Nazareth job centre. *Secondary* primary talents are a little less obvious and a lot less useful and include creativity, fishing, putting ships into bottles and getting stones out of horses' hooves. We need not concern ourselves with the sadly lesser secondary talents, save to say that they count TV producers, homeopaths and estate agents among their numbers. It is not surprising, then, that an innateophile – usually male – would relish his moments of sheer delight, which usually come to him when his talents are pointed out to another man by an envious wife with phrases like '*You* never lift a finger!' or perhaps 'Why can't you do something useful like build your own five-storey extension?' (If it is a mother-in-law doing the pointing out, then the trigger phrases might even be a bit on the cutting side). The agreeable innateophile might attempt to damn the other with faint praise, insisting 'not to worry, a village of thirty-odd inhabitants like this one will always need brand consultants!'

[innatus, innate]

§

Iuvenophilia: delight in one's youth.

As Tom Stoppard once said, 'age is a very high price to pay for maturity'. This is a truism known all too well to the iuvenophiliac, who loves to point out at every opportunity, the ASC* of everything you do. They went out: you stayed in. They watch *Skins*: you watch *Midsomer Murders* (and enjoy it!). They got through several packets of Mates last night; you got through some back issues of *People's Friend*. *Iuvenophilia* is all too common these days, when even the most traditional bastions of our heritage feel the need to rebrand themselves. Radio 4 Extra introduces 'Archers' Nights!'; the *Daily Telegraph* stoops to 'Innit?' in its 'Comment' column; and *The Lady* rebrands itself to *Skirt*. Thank goodness, then for *Iuvenophilia adversa*, a counter strain that has St Dorothy of Parker as its patron (motto *Ante sus, margeritae*). These people delight in the wielding of age as experience and are always the first to smile and point out their subject's total ignorance of the existence of *Marine Boy*. Indeed, a true author's story which may be relevant came when *Doctor Who* was brought back to TV and was hailed an immediate success. The question 'So, who's your favourite Doctor?' was greeted by one iuvenophiliac with the answer 'What do you mean, favourite? Are you saying there has been more than one?'

* age-sensitive content

[iuventus, youth; ante, before; sus, swine; margerita, pearl]

Lardamicophilia: delight in playing sport with a less fit person.

Related to *Turpamicophilia* (qv), this involves the relishing of a sporting fixture with a less-than-able match. Particular delights include manoeuvres such as the Submarine (in which the fitter partner seems to be on a losing path before suddenly coming through to win in the end) and the Leeds United (a fairly unpleasant exhibition match wherein the fitter player toys with their prey). Some say this pleasure is heightened to almost sexual levels if there is a genuine chance of death through heart failure during matches.

[lardium, fat: amicus, friend]

ʒ

Lavacophilia: delight in being on holiday. Today's lavacophiliacs take their pleasure largely in their imagination, as they seek to picture the scene which might ensue when their postcard arrives at its destination.* The tableau should be one of overcast office drudgery, preferably on a Monday, wherein their missive appears like a shining beam of pure Caribbean light. In terms of their weapon of the choice, lavacophiliacs know no shame: the postcard need not display anywhere they have necessarily visited, but merely the best places on offer, those most similar to *Fantasy Island*, arrived at by *Love Boat*, in terms of their utopian photogenics.

Militant lavacophiliacs will buy postcards a year in advance, safe in the knowledge that they can be sent even if they have ventured no further than the 'English Pub and Guest House' just outside Calais, very handy for the booze-cruise Mammoth. It is worth noting that Saint Judith de Chalmers is discredited as the patron saint of holidaymakers as the last thing in the world they espouse is a cry of 'Wish you Were Here': it's more 'Glad I am Here' with a touch of associated 'and that you're not'. A related delight is

Vacophilia lingua nova where one relishes copying out the instructions from the holiday sun cream bottle in the native language onto the postcard home in order to mystify.

* Note, the postcard is the calling card of choice for the lavacophiliac. Modern-day attempts to dent its popularity by way of email, blog or even, heaven forbid, one's own YouTube channel – what manner of devil's own jiggery-pokery is that? – are not for the lavacophiliacs. Guarantee of delivery prior to one's return, therefore, is essential and many are willing to pay significantly over the odds, to the point of foreign DHL accounts, to achieve their goal

[laudare, to praise; vacato, freedom]

༄

Legumaphilia: delight in reading over someone's shoulder.

The collective noun for a group of legumophiliacs must surely be a 'Tube', for the London Underground system is their natural habitat. The sardinesque nature of the Tube makes is not simply *ideal* as a stomping ground but pretty much *de rigueur*. Even the advent of free newspapers didn't check the growth of this delight, with sufferers happy to sport the latest free sheet under their arm as they smile sweetly at the person with whom they are virtually sharing tonsil space and continue to read *the same paper* over their shoulder. On overland commuter trains, the practice has spread not just to newspapers but to work documents. *Legumaphilia cula tota* is seen by many sufferers to be perfectly valid, considering that the person whose documents they are reading has just felt it equally valid to share a loud conversation with

'Janet' about exactly who will be made redundant in the New York office.

[legere, to read; umerus, shoulder; totus, complete; culus, arsehole]

Lentophilia: delight in filibustering.

Eeyore would make an ideal mascot for the lentophiliac community, were it not for the fact that he was not, as such, a lentophiliac himself. Eeyore was slow, admittedly, but do not let the etymology of this word fool you into thinking that this is all about speed. It is not. It's about power. The lentophile adores the attention created following their filibustering delaying tactic, the small eye of a gathering storm which appears to be hovering over them. It could be something as low key as a spouse getting ready upstairs or it could be something as huge as an all-party filibuster in the House of Commons, the pleasure is still the same: *they* can't continue… until *I* have done what *I* am doing! Therefore I am in charge.

The lentophile's demeanour often differs sharply from our own in a number of ways: they have an unusual feel for detail. Indeed, they are prepared to go into plenty more detail than they were yesterday, when they themselves were in a hurry. They also have an increased awareness of the world around them and are perfectly happy to spend time pointing it out, in however child-like a way they might. 'I will be there any… moment… now. Oh, look – *tractor*!'

[lentus, slow]

Libevophilia: delight in displaying books.

To the libevophiliac, a book is a brand. Baudelaire's *Les Fleurs du Mal* is their Nike. *The Scarlet Letter* is their Mulberry. They almost ecstatically delight in other people's *glimpsed* sight of their books, as might the teenager the exposed band of his YSL boxers. Libevophiliacs come in two varieties: those who profess to *Libevophilia maxima* and those who simply have the more common strain *Libevophilia mensa*. *Maxima* sufferers hanker after, and usually achieve, the full-scale library wall, lined with their superior knowledge. Sorry, lined with their books. If they can run to a ladder on wheels, they will die happy. Their life is there, resplendent for all to see.

Libevophilia mensa is a shorter-term, albeit often more virulent, strain showing itself in a desire to 'strew'. Delight is taken in strewing carefully chosen books on one's coffee table, while carefully removing previous 'strewings' lest they ruin the scene. Julian the doctor, who loves am-dram is coming round? Rattigan might be a good strew. Dave the scientist? Try the odd Dawkins. Vicar on the way? 'Oh, that, Vicar, is that still around? Just finished it. The life of Charles Taze Russell. Quite diverting. Borrow it if it interests. More tea?' Perfect.

[liber, book; evidens, visible]

Libresophilia: delight in taking the free trial.

The full kennel name should read 'delight in taking the free trial and cancelling before the paying period'. This very modern pleasure would not have existed a century earlier when the old maxim 'There is no such thing as a free lunch' was undoubtedly true. Now, in the age of people power, if Mammon is not a changed beast then at least it is wearing shorts to the office and the god of Groupon leads us through the retail wilderness. Libresophiles are signatories to the code of buy now, don't pay later. They sign up for free offers with a self-satisfied smile and a note written into their kitchen wall planners to 'Make call and cancel house insurance offer', delighting in the knowledge that they have played the system in a small way. Creatives, single dads and Geminis beware: the note in the wall planner will not work for those such as you because you do not check your wall planners and therefore end up paying for the full monty.

A true libresophile is easy to spot. Their electronic inbox fills up every two to three days with all the different shades of email offers (Groupon, Wowcher, freeloadingbastard.com etc). Their garage never contains a car as it has been remodelled with extra shelving for offer items. They are also the only people prepared to produce a voucher code printout at Claridges.

[liber, free; res, things]

Limenophilia: delight in keeping someone at the door.

Curious one this, afflicting more people now than ever before. In a previous era, keeping anyone standing at the door while you talked to them would have been unheard of. Even in the war years, when men were at the front and visitors were screened for being potential Nazi invaders, one would still be ushered into the parlour with the best plates before you could say '*Guten Morgen*'. Nowadays, in an age when nobody 'just pops round' and you can have a doctor's examination by text, limenophiliacs appear to outnumber others by three to one. They simply adore holding even dearest friends in a doorstep tractor-beam, happy to discuss anything up to and including personal financial details without so much as letting them into the hall. Rain, wind, snow – it all adds to the delight. Occasionally, they will allow people into the kitchen, but only to enjoy the delight of having a 'standing' conversation, never once proffering even a tall stool, despite the fact that their visitor had to break up his journey in Carlisle, what with the blizzard and all. One further strain should be identified, namely *Limenophilia res publica*, afflicting 100 per cent of the sane population. Here, an MP is held in the doorstep tractor-beam while the homeowner takes particular pleasure in explaining why they will *not* be voting for them, doling out a verbal whipping the like of which will mean they never return.

[limen, threshold; res publica, politics]

Linguaphilia: delight in not comprehending a perfectly intelligible foreigner.

It is said that Capuchin monks were keen travellers. They would travel everywhere quickly (espresso) and always with a gun at their side (shots) sometimes very far afield. On one fateful occasion, they reached Latvia, where they singularly failed to make themselves understood. Eventually, a small diplomatic incident occurred while they were trying to order double-shot lattes all round but managed to insult the local royal family instead. Ever since, so Italian legend has it, whenever a cappuccino is ordered, there will always be a linguaphile around to insist he hasn't a clue what anyone is saying. Whether it be on the Champs Elysées or round the corner from the Trevi Fountain, linguaphiles still recite the Capuchin motto *Ignoran bliss est*: Ignorance is bliss. They are very easy to identify in the wild, often clustering in restaurants, overpriced motorway service stations and children's fairgrounds. The key test as to whether you are dealing with a linguaphile is to point to a coffee, then hold up one finger. If the person looks at you, hands held apart, shrugs his shoulder and shakes his head, he is a seasoned linguaphiliac.

[lingua, language]

Locluxophilia: delight in witnessing someone who has not bought a ticket being discovered.

Without a murky shadow of doubt, *Locluxophilia* is one of the purest, sheerest, most unadulterated pleasures in the book. This is in part because there is absolutely nothing to do on the part of the practitioner. *Locluxophilia* strikes in the form of a spectacle staged for your indulgence. So, to the players. They include A Person in Search of a Quiet Life (as Pirandello might have called them) – just one out of an entire carriage of anonymous travellers. Two people in search of a quiet life is a possible, but rare event. Entering from stage left, a Ticket Collector, sometimes a number, streaming into the carriage in waves, like waiters marshalled at a formal dinner, fanning out to cover maximum ground. One, though, is enough. At this point, without fanfare or Shakespearean chorus, the show has begun. The locluxophile can sit back in their chair and simply watch the story unfold. Sometimes it's nice to scan and try to discover the Baddie just as you would in an Agatha Christie novel. Is the Chap with the Folding Bike looking a little nervous? Is the Woman with the Hemp Cloth Bag who seems to be asleep, actually asleep? (That's never going to work! Wonderful.)

And then suddenly, the action begins behind you, like a Howard Brenton play bursting into action on separate stages, and you feign a stiff neck to catch a glimpse through the seats. If it is simply a wrong ticket then, well, the entertainment will be short, although some fun might be wrung out of it. For the *grande spectacle* one needs to hear a great dramatic line: 'Did you know it was an offence to travel without a valid ticket, sir?' will suffice. Suddenly the carriage is a little hushed, save for the two people seated next to the cogecolloquophiliac (qv). Now we are in the heart of the play. No ticket! Splendid. He ran for the train, he replies. The entire carriage's internal monologue choruses a collective 'Yeah, *right!*'

At this point, a wonderful sense of suspense begins to build. The ticket collector does his best, like a gameshow host, not to reveal what his next move will be. Will he enforce the full fare? Will he show mercy? If only he would adopt the gladiatorial thumbs up or down system, it would be so much more fun. By now, the locluxophile is near to a trouser accident with hidden joy. They are even considering taking out their mobile to take a picture. The rest of the carriage, an indeterminate number of locluxophiles among them, are still silent as the collector makes his decision and the show draws to a close. The locluxophile is impassive, the collector has moved on, the victim is embarrassed: everyone is happy.

Locluxophilia illustra is a very rare pleasure indeed, which may only happen once in a lifetime. For the character at the centre of your 'train play' to be someone famous is a truly *recherché* amusement. The author can verify this. Without mentioning any names, he was once ringside at what might have been called *The Last Time I Saw My Ticket*. Sadly, and perhaps due to the significance of the central character, it did not extend to the *grande spectacle*. Another day, perhaps.

[locus, spot; lux, light; illustra, famous]

Lujocophilia: delight in a deep understanding of a particular technology.

Not to be confused with secringeniophiles (qv), lujocophiles don't necessarily like to surprise with their knowledge, but they do adore demonstrating a level of completism that is beyond their fellow guests. I say 'guests', advisedly, because the primary stomping ground of the lujocophile is the dinner or drinks party. 'Technology' in this instance is generally presumed to mean those areas of emerging or fast-moving scientific development, possibly medical, that baffle mere mortals. It does not include areas such as foundation depths necessary for shale in park and ride car parks, sales of kitchen sink ring seals, nor rodent extermination. If you encounter a completist in any of these areas (scientific name 'bore') then it is advised you shoot first and ask questions later. Lujocophiles can often lure in unsuspecting dunderheads with an oversimplification to get them interested – 'Bluetooth…it works just like a ham sandwich, really' – which they then expand to include explanations with which the likes of Foucault would have struggled. Nevertheless, a good lujocophile will keep you enthralled with their knowledge, dispelling myths and breaking down secret walls like a Magic Circle refugee. After all, you being enthralled is the heart of their pleasure.

---

[*] Wally Shelf calls this the 'Jesus' manoeuvre, after the way in which all Christian broadcasters will bring any banal story back to Jesus while doing *Thought for the Day*. For example, '…and you know that tin of peas that I forgot to get from Asda… *that's just like Jesus*!'. See: *Naught for*

the Day: Why Jesus Always Comes Down for Breakfast, Wally Shelf, OUP
(Ollerton University Press)

[ludo, play; joculator, joker; nuntia, news]

Luxophilia: delight in over-decorating the outside of your house at Christmas.

Perhaps luxophiliacs were kept in the dark, in a cupboard under the stairs when they were children. If so, why has Harry Potter not shown an overriding desire to festoon Hogwarts with flashing ropelights and ladder-climbing neon Santas? Or did JK Rowling suppress publication of *Harry Potter and the January Electricity Bill?* Maybe luxophiliacs simply didn't celebrate Christmas anywhere near enough early on and so are making up for it, big time.

Ostensibly, the person who decorates their house in enough bulbs to light up Ellesmere Port does so 'for charity', usually. Of course, they are fooling no one. With a carbon footprint bigger than Belgium – and, according to the local paper 'now in its 35th amazing year and this time using a scaffolding framework to extend upwards' – the lit-up house is surely all about the owner. It's a desperate cry to get on the map – literally, considering it is visible from space and a danger to aircraft. It is Edison meets Lourdes and, if it is next door to you – bang! That wasn't the sound of a lightbulb popping. That, so says the holy *Daily Mail*, was the neighbourhood going.

[lux, light]

Magnaluxophilia: delight in not turning off your high-beam headlights.

A potentially lethal delight which stems from sheer selfishness, this philia is only set to expand as more and more councils choose to turn off their road lights at night. Many magnaluxophiliacs, or people who have a fear of leaving the middle lane of a motorway,* are thought to develop a love of the in-car Super Troupers after a disproportionate amount of their time is spent driving at night – mainly because their phobia extends their journey time by some hours. This means they are, by default, nocturnal. What started as mere self-protection eventually changes into an almost vigilante-style, illuminating attack on all oncoming traffic. Some take their delight to higher levels and attach safari-style roof lights, operated via their sunroof, in order to simulate an Oscar film premiere and rain down air-raid style search beams on unsuspecting motorists. Or did I dream that?

Modern Phobias, Tim Lihoreau, one of the few titles in these notes *not* made up.

[magnus, large; lux, light]

§

Magnordophilia: delight in ordering big when someone else is paying.

One of the group of unspoken philias, *Magnordophilia* is said to have originated in Detroit in the early 1900s when Henry Ford was entertained by local council officials. So the story goes, having been invited to town for a free lunch, the young, thrusting businessman duly over-ordered wildly, encouraged to do so as much by the sommelier as by the chef. When he awoke next morning, he is said to have discovered that he had, at some point in the evening, signed a contract agreeing to move his entire production to the city. Whether this is true or not, a magnordophile neither knows nor cares. They are too busy disguising their philia to make sure it goes unnoticed. The standard call of the majormanophile, 'We're not having starters, are we?' invariably forces the answer 'Of course, we must' and is just one culinary weapon in the free-luncher's armoury. Their secret weapon, and chief delight, is known to practitioners as the Secret Culinary Unloading Device (SCUD) in which they reveal a previously unknown food allergy or preference at the last minute, just as the waiter has taken all other orders, which forces them to have the expensive option from the specials board. Parfait!

[magnus, large; ordo, order]

§

Magonchophilia: delight in playing music too loud.

In Cato's epic Spanish-period poem '*Non Iam*', he mentions an unruly friend who 'has too much sea in his ears' ('*nimium mari in aures ejus*'). This refers to the ancient practice of holding shells to one's ears to 'hear the sea'. Some younger people were allegedly not content with holding one shell, but held two, one to each ear. Magonchophiliacs are thought to derive their name from this practice of 'loud shelling' (*magna conchis*) which continues today in the form of playing music too loud in their headphones. Deliberately. The magonchophiliac is undaunted by threats of hearing loss in much the same way as a smoker is undererred by the increasingly worrying legends on the cigarette packet, such as 'Smoking Can Lead to Gravitational Collapse and Bring About an Infinite Spacetime Curvature'. They adore the selfishness of their environment-obliterating music. They care not what words are being mouthed, save if they were to be 'There is an articulated lorry steaming towards you from the rear – please move a little to your left'. (Just in case, most have learnt to lip read this particular phrase). Chief of the heavenly pleasures, though, is the belief that their music is not only being heard, but being frowned upon for its antisocial qualities. And it usually is.

[magno, loud; conchis, shells]

Maldonophilia: delight in the art of deliberately bad gifting.

It may come as a surprise to many readers that such a category of person exists. But ever since he was given a child's Pinky and Perky singalong album called *Kids Love Pinky and Perky* at the age of 15, the author has known about the existence of these sinister people. To be fair, many maldonophiliacs are simply tight. The hideously inappropriate gift they have just given (perhaps a jar of Yorkshire Mixture to an 18 year old about to go off to college) is based on their budget and is the most forgiveable form of *Maldonophilia*. Other types are less excusable. There are rich maldonophiliacs who give badly by chance, due to a helpless accident of birth which renders them tasteless. Yes, you must believe that they are human *pabulum*, without flavour or spice, and that they genuinely believed the scented candle and matching porcelain clown set was to die for.

The third variety, however, is the one true maldonophiliac. To be precise, *Maldonophilia vera* is the name of the pleasure afflicting those whose darkest moments are now on display in your living room. Often lady golf captains, they are the type to buy you a Jew's Harp for your 40th birthday; a limited edition Hermès sweater (in order to prove that both money *and* taste are no object); they have even gone to the trouble of deliberately turning a silk purse into a sow's ear by travelling to Murano to bring you back a piece of exquisite blown glass – in the shape of a toilet. These are the people for whom the phrase 'It's the thought that counts' has a very special meaning.

[malum, bad; donum, gift]

ఓ

Malnuntiaphilia: delight in delivering bad news.

Recent surveys in the *Lancer* (not to be confused with the *Lancet*) surprised many when they seemed to suggest that 70 per cent of malnuntiaphiliacs were boarding school teachers. The closest group in terms of size was that of British middle managers. In both instances, though, it is thought that the common factor is that both groups occupy the position, effectively, of a sort of tap: the funnel through which *all* news has to pass, and therefore, effectively, what researchers came to term 'the God of news'. The malnuntiaphile in action is a sight to behold. Gone are the rules of getting straight to the point. Instead, in comes a sort of toying with ones prey, a cruel trickle of hints and slow-release information, before the final dagger is inserted with a twist. *Malnuntiaphilia* is not to be confused with the older, often northern habit of announcing the death of friends (*Mornuntiaphilia*, qv).

[malus, bad; nuntia, news]

Ƨ

Maloretophilia: delight in being on a fast train as it whizzes through a station.

If *Malnuntophilia* (qv) is potentially the longest in the book in terms of its gestation period, then surely maloretophilia is the shortest. Even one stop before, when the train driver has just announced that the train will not be stopping at the next stop, sufferers have not yet begun to feel even a hint of *Maloretophilia*. It is only when they are experiencing what is, literally, the rush of the moment when the train whooshes through the unfortunate station that they realise they are loving every millisecond. Veterans have even been known to raise both hands, as if on a roller coaster. One potential side effect can be voluntary whiplash, as some unseasoned maloretophiles seek to push their noses up against the window and quickly dash their head from side to side – an attempt to get a good visual lock on the outraged faces of would-be passengers reaching for their briefcases and staring bemusedly at the train indicator board.

[From Male loco, recta tempus; wrong place, right time]

Mammophilia: delight in the corporate defence.

There are corporate gifts, corporate boxes at the Opera House and corporate manslaughter charges, so it is fitting that there should be an area of *Schadenfreude* that is corporate too. That said, although the delight enjoyed here is most certainly a corporate one – for example, the eloquent almost Baudelairean line on an official corporate reply, telling you that the huge multinational you have unwittingly chosen to do business with 'is not able to authorise' your request – the enjoyment is enjoyed by individuals. For all corporate defences, while existing to further the causes and limit the responsibilities of the corporations themselves, are also enjoyed on a daily basis by the employees who put them into operation. Indeed a standard 'I'm sorry, I'm not allowed to put you through to my supervisor', while being a common way of limiting the escalation of complaints, is also immediately enjoyed by the person reading the said line from the screen. That period where you follow up with 'Hello… Hello, I'm sorry, is there *anyone* there?' is almost certainly the moment during which these particular mammophiles put you on mute to tell their friends 'I just told him I wasn't *allowed* to put him through to a supervisor!' Cue peals of hooting laughter.

Mammophiles exist today more than they ever did. They gather in clusters ('call centres', they term them) and work in groups ('whoops', they term them), practising their delights daily before going home to their partners, who regale them with woeful tales of how they have been on the phone to the council all day.

There is a delightful true tale of Messrs Frank Muir and Dennis Norden, who, as writers for radio, regularly found themselves at the mercy of one famous corporate beast, namely the BBC contracts department, which was wont to reply to many of their requests with a standard letter saying 'I'm sorry. We do not have any mechanisms in place to deal with your request.' One day, they found themselves in receipt of a letter which informed them that they had been paid incorrectly, and that they had, in fact, received a much larger payment than they were warranted. Please, the letter said, could they return the payment ASAP. Muir and Norden are reputed to have sent a letter back in reply which simply said: 'I'm sorry. We do not have any mechanism in place to return your cheque. Yours…'..

[Mammon, god of greed]

ک

Manavophilia: delight in nursing a drink to use the free wi-fi.

There's being tight and there's *Manavophilia*. While they are undoubtedly fruits of the same tree, they are very different in sweetness and intensity. A manavophile is perfectly prepared to buy their way into an establishment with an overpriced vessel of caffeinated frothy milk. From then on, though, they treat it very much as one might treat the entrance fee at a holiday resort: they're not paying for anything else. When they have drunk half their drink, they are 'cup half-full' people. When they have drunk *all* their drink, they are *still* 'cup half-full' people, their sole intention to maintain their wi-fi connection. Occasionally, you will find the odd common or garden tight-arse maintaining that they are merely manavophiles. Signs are a tendency to not carry money, to wear their spectacles on their forehead and to exhibit a total lack of interest in the internet. Not to be confused with plexisophiles (qv) or strictophiles (qv).

[manere, to remain; avius, out of the way]

᛭

Manifevelspecexparteverescon-sequinopinatasemeritemandomiophilia: delight in the dubious appearance of symptoms which result in an impromptu day off.

To cut to the chase and hone this definition further, this is the everyday delight known as 'pulling a sickie'. It is a simple pleasure, enjoyed by millions of workers who can be split into two categories: a) those convinced that their down-at-heel servitude and ever-lengthening hours are making them less able to conduct wholesome or meaningful lives outside the office and therefore feel compelled to recharge their batteries and redress the balance in some small way, and b) skivers. Though differing somewhat in credo, both categories seem to ultimately take the same course of action. If done correctly, a pleasurable period of either daytime TV or DVD box sets, blankets and comfort food ensues. Hull poet Philip Larkin left the following poem, scribbled on the Playmate of the Month pages of the May '68 edition of *Playboy*, among his personal effects, leading biographers to rewrite their biographies to include *M'ophilia*:

> He screws you up, your chief, your boss,
> F for 'file your life away',
> Don't grit your teeth: get even. Floss!
> *Detra'aeger!* Every day.

It should be noted that the sense of comfort time is essential to genuine *M'ophilia*. Many self-proclaimed m'ophiles turn out, under closer scrutiny, to be no more than wasters. Thankfully, with almost medical levels of all-round technological life-monitoring and the pioneering work of social initiatives such as *CCTV Cheaters Caught on Camera*, these people are now being exposed, leaving the pleasures of

Columbo, closed curtains and comfort time to true m'ophiles.

* literally, pull a sickie

[manifestatione vel speciem ex parte vero res consequentes inopinata sed merita tempus manere domi: manifestation or appearance of potentially partially true or untrue symptoms which result in an unexpected but rewarding period of stay at home.]

§

Maximentophilia: delight in being 'well-endowed'.

The easiest way to delight in the greatness of one's front fixtures is to be around those less fortunate and simply flaunt it. In changing rooms, therefore, you will find practitioners of all shades and hues* resplendent in their nakedness, while others around them cling nervously to their towels. Outside the changing room, maximentophiliacs pop up everywhere, no pun intended. Their classic stance is with one leg resting on a low rock or stool, so as best to display themselves. Tighter clothing can be favoured but not in all cases.

* Some delight in their length, others their girth, hence the precise definition of this philia. All too many times it is misdiagnosed.

[maximus, maximum; mentula, penis]

§

Maxipilophilia: delight in looking good.

Never tell a maxipilophiliac about the provenance of the word *Maxipilophilia*. They will almost certainly be put off their passion for life. It is said to have got its unique, seemingly *non sequitur* name from the early cave paintings found in Chauvet, France, which some scholars think make clear that those people who were the hairiest were considered the most attractive. Regardless of the word's origins, the maxipilophiles of today are separated from the merely vain by dint of their approach to others. For it is not simply looking good that is enjoyed by these preening practitioners; it is those around them looking bad that they seek. The declension goes 'I look (good), You look (bad), He/she looks (at me)'.

The maxipilophile man likes to stick out in a crowd, so long as the crowd are made plain in his company. Vain folk love themselves. Maxipilophiles love the fact that others love them. The most common and easiest arena for today's maxipilophile is the beach, where, with 90 per cent of people looking fat or pale, or fat and pale, they are able to shine. Sometimes literally. Models, with their 'catwalk' theatre, have a harder job: not only is the competition stronger, but they are by their very nature, ten times less likely *ever* to find a rival attractive. Hardest of all arenas, though, must be behind the counter at McDonalds. These poor two- and three-star Johnnies are possibly the world's saddest ever victims of corporate clothing, making *Maxipilophilia* there virtually unknown.

[maxima, most; pilosa, hairy]

Mecutempophilia: delight in going to the toilet to read.

There exist, allegedly, people who cannot believe that *Mecutempophilia* actually exists. Queen Victoria was one, apparently: if she ever read on the throne, it was certainly not that type of throne. Non-believers are perfectly happy to accept the existence of a Toilet Duck, therefore, but not a Toilet Book. Ancient Romans, however, had no such reticence, being a bunch of big-time mecutempophiliacs: scholars even suggest that the symbols for 'one' and 'two' preceding many of Pliny's works meant that they were written in specific lengths for toilet consumption. Today, the further north you head, the more often you are likely to see someone sloping off, *Daily Express* rolled under the arm, bound for some quality crappertime. The modern mecutempophile finds his world opened up to him by the wonders of the iPad, to the extent that many husbands have been falsely reported missing, even searches commenced, only for them to slope out of the WC some hours later, with a vacant look and a nonplussed 'What? What is it?'

[meum, my; cunio, defecate; tempo, time]

Mefamaphilia: delight in being recognised.

It must surely be more than simple convenience that the Latin word for fame, *fama*, is also the Latin word for infamy. Mefamaphiliacs often show themselves apart from merely 'those who are famous' with one intriguing tendency. Famous types may constantly suffer from being approached with the now almost clichéd line 'Excuse me, but haven't I seen you somewhere on television?' Mefamaphiliacs, however, tend to invert the process, approaching all and sundry with the question, 'Excuse me, but haven't you seen *me* somewhere on television?' When genuinely approached in the street, they simply cannot prevent the smug smile, tight lips and nodding admission of '*Mea culpa*, darling!' Sometimes, seasoned mefamaphiles will bother to fake a slight displeasure at being recognised, while maintaining a Machiavellian hand on the conversational tiller to make sure the moment doesn't pass all too soon. As they themselves are prone to saying, 'Fame is the spur'. If only they had bothered to read on in Milton's telling quote: to the bit that says 'That last infirmity of noble mind'. Ah, if only they *could* scorn this particular delight.

[mei, me; fama, fame]

ʒ

Melanteophilia: delight in being better than the previous person.

Though *Melanteophilia* can strike in any walk of life, it appears to be most common among CEOs of large multinationals. Taking on the top job in a previously failing firm with a turnover the size of a small country's GDP comes with so many opportunities to fail that it is hardly surprising that 'being better than the last guy' has its own medical definiton. So many lives depend on them for their funding that it isn't odd to find these driven, obsessive and (let's not deny it) anal people enjoying their own success. In some instances, with already successful firms, they have had to live with up to a year of being told that their success could still be down to the last chap, so they're definitely going to be a little smug and take that two-page puff piece in *Intelligent Life*, if you don't mind.

Melanteophilia can also strike further down the pay-scale, particularly where ageing staff have been replaced by younger, thrusting models with go-faster stripes. Replaced also is the gentle self-deprecation which 'old Ken' brought to the job, and in comes the post-Thatcher generation's inbuilt trumpet, self-blown so often (at every opportunity, in fact) that it is hard to actually tell where the good job begins and where the self-marketing ends. A particularly virulent, if intemittent strain, is *Melanteophilia maritus temporaria*. This affects second husbands (the philia gets more pronounced for each further husband taken) who enjoy being told that they are, shall we say, able to take their spouses on longer journeys in the trouser department. The intermittent nature of the delight is purely down to trust, especially when the image of the former partner, a seven-foot Olympic oarsman who left to pursue a career as a lumberjack, comes into their minds. At the most inopportune times.

[melius, better; ante, before; maritus, husband]

Melectiophilia: delight in being better-read than others.

Most melectiophiliacs stalk their prey with quotations. Dinner parties are, once again, the favoured stomping grounds. Here's how the melectiophiliac gains maximum pleasure. Once the dinner is in place, they throw in the odd litmus-test quotation. A classic one, and adaptable to just about every situation, would be: 'Ah, yes, damn with faint praise, eh?' At this point the melectiophiliac might head off to the kitchen in pursuit of after-dinner mints, but keeping a keen ear on the ensuing discussions. If he hears anything which sounds anything like 'And assent with civil leer', then he soon realises his game is not yet commenced and he must lob in another quote. If, however he is greeted with silence from his guest then perhaps there is some melectiophile pleasure to be had, and he must simply tease it out. On the other hand, if he scores a direct hit and the response is something on the lines of: 'Absolutely! I blame the parents!' then he knows he has hit the jackpot.

'Pope', retorts the melectiophile.

'No, I don't blame the Pope,' comes the reply, 'what's the Pope got to do with it?'

'No, Pope. The poet', he continues.

'Ah, yes, Benedict. I'd heard he was a bit of a poet.'

'I think that's Rowan Williams.'

'Really? Not surprised he's trying poetry. He hasn't done anything worth watching since *Good Morning, Vietnam!*'

Scrumptious stuff that quite makes you forget the mints. Food enough.

[melius, better; lecio, read]

ॐ

Melesophilia: delight in meeting a friend who has aged badly.

This is a lovely one. Although it can manifest itself in many ways, it takes its name from the most startling version of the species, namely meeting a friend whose hair has not been kind to them. Translated literally it comes out as 'fear of the badger' and stems from its first sighting in Ovid:

Post percutere de manibus,
Conspexit in capite melium,
Risui ut effundu.

The sad black-and-white head rug is certainly not confined to days of yore, and many is the old friend who has not just enjoyed his moment of *Melesophilia* but also, perhaps, used it to even up a previously unbalanced relationship. Take, for example, the case of the old college chums meeting again after fifteen years. Back then, A was fit, flirty and full of himself. B, on the other hand, was flabby, furtive and failing more than a little. Seeing the spectacular lines of white and grey now streaking like zephyrs across A's bonce, B is an instant melesophile. It starts with the occasional, deliberately ill-timed glance upwards, while holding tight in a prisoner's handshake. If the former relationship was particularly uneven, verging on the dominant, an old college photo might even be retrieved and the obvious pointed out, *molto fortissimo*: 'Ah, look, do you remember? That's me… and that's you with the jet back hair!' In extreme cases, a cap might be offered, under the pretext of 'covering up in this sun'. Everyone will realise too, don't worry, that you don't normally shake your hair like Jennifer Aniston in a L'Oreal advert as you have been doing on this occasion. But still. You're worth it.

* 'He having been about to shake hands caught sight of what appeared to be a badger on his head and, yea, laughed he like a drain.' From Ovid's *Historia Duo Milia Graecorum*.

[meles, badger]

Mendicaphilia: delight in lying to cold callers.

If Saint Ignatius Loyola had been around today, he would surely have understood. The Grand Equivocator would no doubt endorse the pleasures of the mendicaphiliac, who exact their revenge on ubiquitous cold callers by the means of total bullshit. They tend to start small, perhaps by trying a fictional greeting on pickup ('Hello, Saint Fellatio's School for Wayward Girls, who's calling?', etc). If buoyed by their early success (many a mendicaphiliac's career has been cut short when forced to utter the follow-up line 'Oh, hello Vicar…') they might continue on the road to deception. After all, this is a cold call, thus named because it is a lifeless corpse of a communication, and they did not invite it into their home. So, with a gentle smile, they do not own up to being the homeowner. That is step two.

Then they go a step further. Ah, no, sorry, they don't know when the owner will be home because (a) they are only lodgers, (b) they are suffering from temporary amnesia or (c) we are having trouble with our crossed electronic wiring systems and you've actually come through on the fridge. As you see, a mendicophiliac's responses will vary with confidence levels. At the heart of this delicious pleasure is the genuinely held belief that this one of the three occasions when lying is not just perfectly acceptable but recommended. As the saying goes, 'Age and love and cold, cold callers'.

[mendax, lie; dicere, to tell]

ᶘ

Menepisophilia: delight in fooling recipients of email content via title.

It starts as a lesson. A lesson for those people who continually ignore your emails. Indeed, they openly ignore your emails and boast of having done so to canteen friends. To be fair, it's hardly surprising when your email is entitled 'Year Ends, '88–'08, Midlands and East England: All need checking'. Doesn't exactly scream 'open me, read me and run away with me to the Maldives!' So, you dip your first toe in *Menepisophilia*. You send the offender an email labelled: 'That chap you fancy, he just said that you are…'. Not surprisingly, thanks to the Return Receipt (a dark delight in itself) you find that your email is opened.

And so it has begun. Pretty soon you are a fairly active menepisophiliac. You get high on the deceptive contrast that seems to pierce your victims firewall each time. 'Picture of the Boss' is actually 'Forecast Sales for 11/12'. 'Did you leave this in the canteen?' contains 'Names and Addresses of all Clients – please hand-write each one'. And, just for double pleasure, 'Year Ends, '88–'08, Midlands and East England' actually does contain 'what that chap you fancied said about you'. It's a simple, child's delight but writ corporate, to run alongside flirting, phantom emails and adding graffiti saying *'Non est de necessitate quod insanitis operare, sed sicut adiuvans'* to notices. Or is that just me?

[mendacium, lie; epistola, letter; est de necessitate quod insanitis operare, sed sicut adiuvans, you don't have to be mad to work here, but it helps]

ৎ

Meverbophilia: delight in looking great in front of an ex.

This is one of the more transient delights, and not one that can so much be practised as grabbed. Meverbophiles tend to find their pleasures come in moments, which they have to seize. At best, if all goes well, they can approach a potential encounter with preparation, fly in, impress and then fly out again. If all has gone superbly, they might even find

that their ex looked like they'd just got up. Mwah!
Meverbophiles sometimes use an extra weapon,
namely a stooge who might stand in as their arm
candy, further evidence of how well they are doing.
Etymologically speaking, the name has nothing to
do with Dan Maschal's famous tennis catchphrase
but derives from the common cry of the impressed
former love, '*O mea verba, ecce in eo fundus*', the
motto of many a meverbophile the world over.

['O mea verba…', Oh my word; ecce, behold; in eo, on that; fundus, arse]

Mornuntiaphilia: delight in announcing death.

The militant wing of *Malnuntiaphilia* (qv).
A sample conversation might go:

    A: You know Elsie Hedges…

    B: Yes.

    A: …we saw her last Thursday?

    B: Yes.

    A: …and we said how well she looked?

    B: Yes.

    A: …we left her skipping down the road, singing
       'Everything's coming up roses!?'

    B: YES…!

    A: …DEAD!

    B: Noooo!

You know the type.

[mortem, death; nuntia, announce]

Musanglophilia: delight in the crap performance of another country's national anthem.

This is one of those delights made all the more delightful because it can never be proven. Along with waterlogged dressing rooms and insufficient translation, arranging a terrible performance of the opposing country's national anthem is one of those secret weapons which can give a vital edge in any sporting battle. Very often, the speeding up or slowing down of a good anthem – like that of the French – can make all the difference to winning or losing. Similarly, allowing it to be performed by the latest crossover star, possibly even accompanied by a children's choir, can offend a visiting side enough to put them completely off their game. Nothing can beat the wrong speed, though. Or even a number of wrong speeds – speeding up for no reason at good bits and slowing down in others – has been known. Of course, some countries' anthems cannot be made any worse, which is how this philia gained its name.

[musica, music; anglia, England]

Mutophilia: delight in not answering the phone.

A very modern philia, *Mutophilia* is not to be confused with *Occuphilia* (qv). In the days of bakelite, bell-ringing phones, this would have been no delight at all. To leave a phone unanswered then would have been delightful only in the way an incessantly crying baby is delightful. That is, not at all. Much like a Greek deity, hovering above the clouds, looking down on the mortals below, a mutophile enjoys the way his mobile silently flashes at him. Better still is to have it on vibrate, to hear its distressed buzzing and to see it flailing around the desk surface, like a downed insect. All the better to ignore. Essentially, at best mutophiles are procrastinators, at worst ostriches, using technology to help them hide their heads in the sand. And annoy the hell out of the rest of us.

[mutus, mute]

§

Niganimophilia: delight in having mirror-tinted car windows.

Going straight to the nub of this issue, let's talk about superiority. It is the prime motivator for today's niganimophiliacs, who are chiefly drawn from the otherwise seemingly disparate worlds of rap superstardom and presidential protection.[*] The game a niganimophiliac likes to play is simply 'Guess Who?' No different, in many ways, from their childhood games of peekaboo. A large limousine with mirror-tinted windows can't help but pique the interest of passers-by. Certainly, more than, say, a K-reg Toyota Corolla with clear windows might arouse it. What is important to remember about *Niganimophilia* is that you are never quite sure you are seeing it at work. As with secroculophiliacs (qv), nothing is ever fully revealed. You may be witnessing a passing popstar driving in a stretch Merc, number plate TO55€R. Or you may not. It might be his driver using it at weekends to nip the family to DFS. Or it might even be a runaway, the rap equivalent of the Grand National's riderless horse. This is the primary pleasure for a niganimophiliac and can be traced right back to when they used to watch crime series involving interrogation rooms with two-way mirrors.**

* Beyond mirror-tinted windows, earpieces and acronyms are the only other things explicitly shared by both worlds (FBI, Will.I.AM, CIA, MC Hammer etc). Perhaps this connection might merit a costly study by a former poly keen to pick up on bizarre research to get themselves valuable column inches. The name, incidentally, refers to the eyes being the windows of the soul. Only, in this instance, they have shades on.
** Surely 'two-way mirrors' is a misnomer?

[niger, black; anima, soul]

ʬ

Nimbuphilia: to delight in driving wildly through a kerb-side puddle which you know to be too close to a pedestrian.

In part of Scotland, this is still called *drookin' the goose*. The 'drook' or 'drooker' – the driver – has their pleasure magnified by the disparity between their own position and that of the 'goose' – the victim. On the one hand, they can imagine their victim's total drenching, their every pore pooling with rainwater, their sopping clothes clinging to their moistened chests. And on the other, they take equal delight in the fact that they themselves are warm, cosy and serenaded by the most recent cheesy compilation CD given away free with the Sunday papers. Sometimes, a drook will try to convince themselves that they could not *avoid* driving like Jenson Button in a paddling pool. Deep down, though, the merest hint of the Mona Lisa smile on their faces gives away their intent. They loved it.

Some variations occasionally occur, notably the increased delight experienced by numbuphiliacs who can achieve their goal while it is not actually raining – perhaps in that golden period *après le deluge*. Saturating someone who is already soaking wet is one thing, but drenching an unsuspecting punter in their crisp, freshly pressed shirt is, well, quite clearly something else. Some drooks, for appearance's sake, will take steps to avoid soaking unwitting bipeds when they have a passenger in the car. Chronics, however, adore it too much to care. Sod them. Then sodden them.

[nimbus, rain cloud]

§

Niovemophilia: delight in dispelling a myth.

Possibly one of the toughest philias to get a handle on in the entire book and yet, also one of the oldest. *Niovemophilia* stretches back centuries as the name suggests: it derives from those people who would tell children that Jupiter did not exist and that 'no bulls were harmed in the making of this three-week period of rain'. Today, they are still all around us, many of them mingling unnoticed in polite society. They are often hard to spot, with the leaps and bounds made in both skin creams and plastic surgery, and very few nowadays entice people with red apples. They are usually spinsters or Dinkies* who simply can't wait until Halloween each year to spin horror stores like 'There Is No Santa'. Or 'Tooth Fairy, Schmooth Fairy'. Maybe even the worst one, 'There's No Chance of Harry Potter VIII!'

* Double income, no kids

[non, no; Iovem, Jupiter]

§

Nocaeruflavophilia: delight in silencing a politician.

Here is a modern philia for which the remote control might have been invented. To think, back in the 1970s, one had to stand up to turn off a politician if they appeared on television. Now, you can simply set phasers to stun and blip them off. Marvellous. Confirmed nocaeruflavophiliacs often invest in novelty remotes, in order to increase the pleasure. Top of the list is the Harry Potter wand remote, which allows you a satisfying 'Expelliarmus!' before the blathering bore is blown off the face of the earth. Well, of the TV at least. Most follow up with a generic 'And that's telling you!' or some such, just to reinforce the delight. One extreme form exists, *Nocaeruflavophilia physica*, which occurs when you get the rare chance to make your MP disappear in person, namely by closing the door on them during canvassing. The classic manoeuvre here is in pure silence although, if preferred, a firm but smiling 'Not on your nelly!' can be added for deeper joy.

[caerulus, blue; ruber, red; flavus, yellow]

§

Noconcordophilia: delight in being loud during another's hangover.

Let's start this one with a 'control' sentence. At college or university, many people genuinely study. If this sentence a) comes as a shock to you, then you are almost certainly not a noconcordophile. If however, this sentence b) is as obvious as the day is long, then you could well have been, or even still be, a student of the dark art of *Noconcordophilia*. As such, you probably spent your college years genuinely studying. A classic 'trigger' night for noconcordophiliacs might see you, still at your lamplit desk, at 3a.m. At this point, a kebab hits the window. It is A. Pissant, student of beer, trying to attract your attention to let him in. He is, indeed, in a state of inebriation. For the next two hours, despite knowing full well that you have a dissertation on the Enlightened Despots to finish in under three months, he proceeds to monopolise your time between tales of his love for you and attempting to get through to the late night television gaming channels, convinced the answer to the anagram of a famous capital city – OTKOY – is Wigan.

From this point on (or more precisely from the following morning) you are a confirmed noconcordophiliac. As soon as you spot your prey, in his pyjamas, you set to work like a great conductor, the kitchen your orchestra. First you bring in the percussion section: the knives and forks drawer. It is like the *1812* in cutlery form – but not for you; for your victim. Next the wind section, as you open the window, to let in not just the freezing breeze but the workmen drilling outside. Cue the brass as the taps turn, their rumbling, banshee-like wail a testament to not only how many times you have promised yourself you might call a plumber but also, today, your sheer ingenuity. You are like a Boulez, finding wonderful music in all things, and forcing your victim to scamper off back to bed, Red Bull in hand. No matter. The radio comes alive, at a spine-tapping 11.

[concordia, sympathy]

§

Nodicophilia: delight in hanging up on a difficult conversation.

There is a line in the Gershwin brothers' song, *They All Laughed*, which goes:

> They all laughed at Christopher Columbus when he said the world was round.
> They all laughed when Edison invented sound.

Well, sadly nodicophiliacs are not laughing. They have never laughed. Never, that is, until they discovered they actually *were* nodicophiliacs.

To explain, usually a nodicophile finds that the modern world doesn't agree with them. They resent doors no longer being held open, 't's being dropped and, most certainly, denim waistbands worn dangerously low on the buttocks. Most of all, they resent the fact that they are contactable at every second of every minute of the day by their boss – a man they would, in an ideal world, cross the continent to avoid. So, they make up for this by the use of what some call, inexplicably, Edison's Revenge. Yes, the mobile phone can put people in touch, but it can't yet tell them where you are. So, they delight in simply cutting you off.

The modern mobile comes complete with modern excuses – 'it's a very bad line' (seasoned nodicophiles will make sure that they are in the middle of a full sentence when they press the red button: much more authentic that way). Many will use it to avoid having a difficult conversation with their nearest and dearest. Some will use it as a means of a cursory log in ('I did try to call, as you know, but… tsk, we got cut off!') with officialdom. Still others, of course, simply become addicted to the many uses of the practice.

[dicere, to say]

§

Nodonophilia: delight in not contributing to a leaving present but signing the card.

Firstly, let's get one thing straight. Your average nodonophiliac is not simply someone who doesn't want to contribute to a leaving present because they have decided they can't afford it. The medical term for this is a tight-arse. A nodonophiliac, on the other hand, genuinely cares little for the monetary impact or otherwise of the donation. They simply *want* to get away with not contributing. It's a thrill. It's a challenge. If the card is left *with them*, in fact, to complete in their own time, then the bet is off. That's no fun.

The nodonophile will wait until they are in full view. They will toy with the pen and cogitate over exactly what to write in the card, having read what others have written some three times over, commenting 'Oh...I don't know what to put', ever louder each time. Then, when all eyes are on them, they will do what is known in the trade as 'The Eric Morecambe',[*] a move which, in skilful hands, can be a wonderful sight. Holding a two pound coin in one hand just below the opening of the envelope, they flick the envelope base with the other, thus giving the impression that the money has been safely deposited in the bottom: all the while, they cling onto the money in a manoeuvre which might make a member of the Magic Circle proud. If they are feeling particularly bad, they might try The Robert Maxwell,[**] wherein they use a five pound note and 'take some change, if that's ok?' Of course, a skilled nodonophile should be able to withdraw anything up to three times the amount he is seen to put in. Quite a feat.

Special mention should be given to donophiles, the sad and often impoverished alter-egos of this intriguing group. They are the ones who, when the collection for a particularly ill-thought of person raises not even enough to cover the cost of the unamusing, embossed, outsized card, feel that they have to add a hefty subsidy to make sure it doesn't look bad.

* From the December, 1983 issue and "November 1991 issue, respectively, of *CardSharp*, the journal of NADA (Nodonophiliacs Anonymous Defence Association)

[non, not; donare, to give]

§

Noluxarcophilia: delight in not owning a TV.

The extreme far-right wing faction of TV denialism now numbering a handful of librarians, independent publishers and expat classics teachers only over here to sort out their home rental agreements. If they can be caught out – by letting slip that *The One Show* has a different presenter on Fridays, for instance – then they are simply downgraded from 'noluxarcophile' to mere 'arse'.

[lux, light; arcula, box]

§

Nomenophilia: delight in a title before or letters after your name.

The majority of us will never know how we will react when presented with the opportunity to add either a title or a series of letters to our name. Perhaps (a) we will turn the chance down. We might (b) accept graciously, then never mention it again for the rest of our lives, leading many to be unaware of its existence. Of course, it's far more likely that we will (c) blather on for years to anyone who will listen and become complete and utter nomenophiles. From here on in, nomenophiles will pretend they hate the lexical annexe yet include it on every piece of literature they produce, including the note to the binman. *Nomenophilia honoraria*, can even change a person's character overnight as they begin to wonder if they truly *are* gifted in the area of their honorary degree. They only need to remember Kenny Garrett and his honorary degree in music to know how dangerous this can be.

Nomenophilia publica can see people become old before their time in a bid to act like 'veterans', a delight which, while benign, can lead to delusions of national treasure status. As many of us know, the Queen only allows there to be two national treasures at any one time (one male, one female) so, with Stephen Fry and Judi Dench, we have a full complement.

[nomen, name]

§

Nomescrophilia: delight in being asked for your autograph.

Originally considered a form of *Famaphilia* (qv), *Nomescrophilia* is now separated in order to deal more fully with this burgeoning condition. In a world where the last few remaining bookshops on earth seem to sell more pre-signed new books than not, the nomescrophiliac is easily spotted. The two most common positions include the *immota* nomescrophiliac – usually seated behind trestle tables – and the *movendi* nomescrophiliac, the moving variety most often 'glimpsed' emerging from stage doors. I say 'glimpsed' because you could actually study them in almost medical detail, as, depite their cry of, 'Sorry, darlings, but I am in a hurry!' they are moving slowly enough to merit time-lapse photography. Indeed, as well as signing all the 13 autographs, they also managed to sign the map of two German tourists who were only looking for Covent Garden and the name-board being held up by the taxi driver waiting for John Barrowman. It is their dark delight, and can only be stunted by one response after a signing: 'Oi, Janice, don't bother, it's not him!'

[nomine, name; scribere, write]

Noncredophilia: delight in being an unbeliever.

There was a time, in the UK, when you were in the majority as a church-going Christian. No longer. With the Dawkins Dawn (aka, roughly, the Millennium) non-belief is the new black, and governments across the globe are falling over themselves to crush crucifixes and ban burqas. The noncredophile does not wear his delight lightly, buoyed by the groundswell which suddenly sees his team in the ascendancy. Accordingly

he will not hold back with his views, but savour the sheepish replies of his more restrained fellow dinner-party guests. Should he encounter the Vicar, he feels emboldened to take the path of most resistance, like a mountaineer scaling the toughest face, even pointing out the failings of his fellow climbers. 'Come on, Andy, be honest with the Vicar, 'cause you said you thought it was all mumbo-jumbo, didn't you?' Armed with a penchant for science, mental notes from a documentary on the making of *The Da Vinci Code* and a giant hole where his faith used to be, he cherishes the moments when his motley collection of cod facts ('Now, did you know that football is banned in the bible?') can be sprung from their lonely resting place in his brain in order to recruit one more former soul to his cause.
[credo, I believe]

§

Nonexilophilia: delight in inappropriate flirting.

There is a whole raft of flirting that is inappropriate by nature, by dint of its existence. *Nonexilophilia* does not deal with such flirtings, so you can rest assured that the words 'with the babysitter' have now made their only appearance in this definition. Also, for the largely female practice of onward leading, see *Fortanotophilia*. But here we find *Nonexilophilia amica* – deliberately enjoying flirting with a good friend of your partner – and *Nonexilophilia maritus* – with a friend's spouse, usually at a dinner party. In the workplace, where flirting is akin to breathing, gloves often come off to enable innappropriate flirting to reach new levels. *Nonexilophilia magister* is the most well-documented and is not to be confused with 'sleeping your way to the top'. The first has been known to lead to the second, but strictly speaking should not: it is a wholly separate condition, in which the practitioner makes the boss think the second is possible when it is not.

Other workplace strains include *Nonexilophilia seneca*, in which the subject innappropriately flirts with someone far older than them, thus doubling the pleasure. Back in the social sphere, there is one occasional delight which can rear its head when a group of friends maintain a particularly small circle, adding 'star guests' from time to time. It is therefore possible you might occasionally indulge in *Nonexilophilia secretia*, wherein the 'star guest' is at a disadvantage to his fellow diners in being the only one totally unaware that the person flirting with them is a complete a) loser, b) git or c) estate agent.

[auxilio, help; magister, boss]

Nonrenovophilia: delight in a boy being a boy.

Nonrenovophiles see their pleasure not so much as an indulgence as a return to basics. They can reinforce the validity of their views by invoking the austerity age, a need for some sort of halcyon Felicity Kendall-esque

Good Life or even, at a tenuous stretch, they see their position as a wholly necessary counter to the perils of texting, iPods and headphones. For a nonrenovophile, boys should be boys and PC can refer either to a computer or a 1970s copper called Rosie. Their bibles are the recent crop of *How to Climb Trees* manuals and their prey are, usually, other people's children.

Whether or not they grew up learning how to use a carborundum stone to sharpen a pocket knife – and, indeed, many have managed to block out the fact that their parents were hippies who walked naked round the house, popped flower petals into the salad in their school lunchbox and gave them the middle name Shelley – they now believe that being a boy means being a boy. Beware of confusing them with chaophiles (qv) when they buy your boy an air pistol for his birthday. It is not the noise that is the issue: indeed, it was their third choice present only after they had rejected the lasso and the Tomy 'My First Flame Thrower'. Sadly, your child will never find themselves the recipient of Tonka toys because the moment the nonrenovophile does come across these in their local small toy shop which these days mostly stocks twee, mock-Victorian, wooden items (his natural habitat for buying toys is an online shop that caters for armageddon day supplies) they will break down in tears, thumb in mouth, memories flooding back amidst plaintive cries of 'Nanny! NANNY!'

[non, not; renovatus, reconstructed]

Nopertuophilia: delight in finding out your ex's new partner is bad in bed.

What's new… how is the world treating you?
Remember when we… two both were young?
Sorry your new chap's… so badly hung.

These are allegedly the lost words to the song *What's New?*, by Burke and Haggart, and were found amongst Burke's private possessions when his estate was settled in the 1960s. Had Burke used these lines as the turn-around last verse of the song, Sinatra might have sung it quite differently. It might also have done something to raise the profile of nopertuophiliacs everywhere. The definition here is impractically narrow, of course, fixating on the bedroom performance. In reality, nopertuophiles will take their pleasures wherever they can find them – noting that their ex's new partner is a little on the flabby side, their ex's current car is 'oh, still that one', their ex is currently talking to them from the wrong side of the reinforced glass on visiting day. It all adds up. Somehow, though, the real or rumoured disappointing sexual performance of the new guy has stolen the limelight. Some sacked football managers have experienced *Nopertuophilia unelectia*, delight when their replacement has overseen relegation into a lower league.

[non, not; per, through; tu, you; unum, one; electi, chosen]

Nothesophilia: delight in using new technology.

Marketeers use the rather cold title 'early adopter' for those first out of the traps with shiny, new technology. Perhaps that is because labelling them 'spoilt, geeky brats with more money than sense' might either be too long for the focus group sessions or raise a few eyebrows were it to ever leak to the public. Nothesophiliacs come, by and large, from this early adopter category (see *Oporthabophilia*). Commuter trains and coffee shops – ones where the actual word *coffee* does not seem to appear on the menu – are their favoured stomping grounds. Here, they delight in brandishing their latest must-have hardware with a mannered nonchalance that fools none but the spongiest brain. On the outside, to all intents and purposes, they might simply be pulling a dog-eared jotter from their bag before opening it to write. Internally, they are screaming, turning up the dial to 11 to holler 'Can you see me? I've got one of those i-thingies. Yes, yes, the ones you've seen in all the trendy magazines!'

What is crucial here is both the faux lack of interest and the public forum. It's safe to say that not only are they biting their lips to save licking them but also, that using their i-beloved in the privacy of, say, their own utility room on a bank holiday Monday wouldn't have quite the same pull. It does not matter that, in reality, their new toy (and how apt that it often literally *is* the Apple of their i) has been a bit of a disappointment to them. Indeed, were they being honest with themselves (rare) they might even own up to feelings akin to Christmas Day evening for a seven-year-old: yes, absolutely, I did pester for months to get Ricochet Racers, but now the empty inside plastic tray of a selection box somehow holds more allure.

Nevertheless, the frisson a nothesophiliac gains from the peripheral sight of a turning head, or better still a nudge and a wink, is still enough to feed on. Fending off cooing inquiries with the proud smile of an actor doorstepped by a stage-door Johnny, they are happy to work under the spotlight of envious admiration. That is, up to a point. Were the attention to morph into badgering or, worse, a request to 'have a go', then the relationship can sour. Nothesophiliacs are very easy to spot, as they insist on giving themselves away with phrases like 'Sent from my … (insert latest gadget here)' added onto their emails. If they get too unbearable, simply slap them while muttering 'Sent from the palm of my hand'. *Nothesophilia* is occasionally countered by *Pullophilia* – the delight in seeing someone who has adopted technology which proves to be a complete turkey. You sir, with your Betamax video, driving your Sinclair C5: I'm talking to you.

[novum, new; thesauri, treasures; pullum, turkey]

Novaletudophilia: delight in being ill.

It is worth stating, from the outset, that this is not the male affliction of combined infirmity and exhibitionism called Man Flu, known to affect a large percentage of the bloke population at roughly the same time as outbreaks of the common cold among women. In Man Flu, which *Gilbie's Olde Manual of Ruinous Ailmentes and Generale Narks* (1665) describes as 'that maladie whyche shalle be soffered by gentlemen, much as by laydies, all being it at a spoiling ratio of thrice the payn…', the victim tends not to actually enjoy the affliction, being the type of person one might at one point have referred to as a great wet lettuce. The novaletudophiliac differs by dint of the dual-natured aspect of their 'problem'. Yes, they become ill, and yes, they do suffer from a great malady ratio compared to others.

The other side, though, is the need to see someone else inconvenienced by the illness, preferably a work colleague. If the novaletudophile is to suffer the illness, then someone else is to join them in some necessarily unpleasant knock-on effects, often communicated today via email but, if correct procedure be followed, via a phone call. Indeed, there is some evidence to back up contemporary rivals' claims that the full extent of Alexander Graham Bell's famous, historic conversation went something like: 'Mr Watson, come here… I want to see you. I'm not feeling great, so you'll have to do all my work for the rest of the week. So long, sucker!' (although it is very much disputed). Overall, a novaletudophile is almost always genuinely ill and so therefore not a manifevelspecexparteveresconsequinopinatasemeritemandomiophile (qv) even though the watching of

comfort TV and consumption of junk/comfort food
may be common to both.

[valetudo, healthy]

§

Noverconsophilia: delight in
overspending on a spouse's card.

Not to be confused with *Magnordophilia* (qv); it
is the personally related nature of the spend that
delights here. The credit card one is using is that of a
related person, and therefore the money being spent
is justifiable. You two made vows, for heaven's sake,
so you are only enacting the 'for richer, for poorer'
bit. And guess which way round? For optimum
enjoyment, this delight should be enjoyed whilst in
the presence of friends and preferably in some sort of
nightclub environment. To add a further twist, one's
partner might be in sight, able to see you and your
friends raising a glass to his health, without realising
it is his financial health.

Related to this is *Noverconsophilia adolescans*,
a far more dangerous strain which many parents
believe should be reclassified from 'philia' into more
'offence carrying custodial sentence'. Practitioners
here are on a pleasure high, often literally. Their
delight in their posession of a parental credit card is
both real and surreal at the same time, with the added
dimension of its occurrence during holiday season
being a further distraction. It is no coincidence that
many full-blown noverconsophiliacs started out with

copious quantities of alcohol, food and stain remover as their first purchases.

[vero, true; consumus, spending; adolescans, youth]

§

Noviteophilia: delight in not recognising a celebrity.

In days of old, when men were men and dinner had to be clubbed to death, there were far fewer celebrities in the firmament. Even in more recent times, namely the last one hundred years, when numbers did rise, it is thought these smiling cranial air-containers accounted for a mere 0.5 per cent of the population. Possibly less. Today, with parameters having been redefined in the mid- to late-1990s – to include footballers, reality-TV participants, footballers wives, reality-TV participants' wives, soap extras, girls who bared their breasts on the internet, boyfriends of girls who bared their breasts on the internet, husbands of Katie Price, anyone retweeted by Stephen Fry and those people insulted by politicians during an election campaign – that percentage has now risen somewhat, to 95.8 per cent.

Accordingly, *Noviteophilia* is not only on the increase but now almost clinically recommended by doctors. Helpfully, it is much, much easier to pull off too, as the bulk of the targets are now these *nouveaux celebres,* as the French call them: celebrities who, even under the new parameters, still don't merit so much as a Z in the *Guide Alphabetique de Michelin* (this puts them lower down than the equivalent of the Vauxhall Conference league of stardom). As a result, their 'star quality' is much less professional, hence easier to ignore. Real noviteophiles, though, love to ignore the more A-list celebrities, with long-established *amuse-bouches* (much of the vocabulary of the noviteophile is French, some of it culinary) of delight. One such is the simple *voix humaine* (human voice to non-French speakers), the ravishing conversation in which one approaches and asks the A-lister for the time, calling them 'mate' as one departs. The lack of the much longed-for double take is often more than some can bear. Chief among the shady spoils, though, is the *à bout de souffle* (at breath's end), namely proffering them a pen and paper, raising their expectant coy smile then deflating them totally by asking them to draw you directions to a nearby landmark. *Joyeux*!

[Non video te; I can't see you]

§

Occuphilia: delight in 'busying' someone on your mobile.

Not to be confused with *Mutophilia* (qv), this temporal joy is one which can be enjoyed many times a day. On a practical level, it carries with it the double whammy of avoiding a potentially tough conversation and giving one the sense of having swatted a small fly. Various shades of *Occuphilia* exist, from *Occuphilia certanumera*, in which one enjoys refusing the call of a certain person, to *Occuphilia prohiba*, wherein one refuses to talk to someone impolite enough to withhold their number. More common these days is *Occuphilia ignotia*, a rapidly expanding philia in which one enjoys not having to take a call simply because one does not recognise the number. A dubious delight unavailable to us until the mid-1980s.

Just like Madonna.

[occupatus, busy; certum, particular; numerus, number; prohibere, withhold; ignotus, unknown]

ʊ

Oporthabophilia: delight in being an early adopter.

Not to be confused with *Nothesophilia* (qv). Oporthabophiliacs don't enjoy the display of their all-new wares; they simply love the fact that they have them. They are the selfish version of nothesophiliacs, if you like. Practitioners of this dark art drive their loved ones* insane with their compunction to possess the latest gadgetry. They rarely fail in their quest, either. A true oporthabophiliac will not boast, nor will they show off. They will, if they do venture out, simply smile an embarrassed smile, possibly twitch a little, and proceed to fill you in, at length, on the 'latest version' and how it 'walks all over the competition, man. It's in the code, dude, you know, it's in the code!' Don't be put off by the faltering L.A. accent. You aren't mistaken. They *are* from Croydon.

* Although figures produced by the computer industry's most trusted data-crunching companies, New Era Research Developments of San Francisco, suggests that a huge 98 per cent of oporthabophiliacs *don't actually have*

loved ones. Not even close! Unless you count Madame de La Main et sa cinq belles filles.

[oportet, must; habere, to have]

ς

Opulophilia: delight in the knowledge that someone earns less than you.

Also known, particularly in the Square Mile five-a-side leagues, as 'Brunei are playing at home to Bangladesh'. This is very common in the family scenario, where financial information can occasionally seep out through a well-intentioned comment, or gush like blood in a Tarantino film courtesy of a drunken gaffe at a family get-together. In the work environment, where a disclosed salary is rarer than an invitation to a sleepover at Anne Frank's, the delight is intensified anything up to 100 times (the precise amount being a delicate algorithm dependent on how much the differential in wage was, multiplied by the extent to which it was unexpected).

Brunei rarely play at home to Bangladesh, ironically, when the wage difference is utterly enormous – that is to say, for example, you are unlikely to hear a Rupert Murdoch labouring the size of his bank balance to his chauffeur. This rule changes, however, if such a position were to be unexpected. For example, if a national newspaper were to leak the salaries of BBC presenters, revealing that Chris Moyles earned more than the Director General, then, were he an opulophiliac, it might be well within Moyles' rights to bask in the knowledge. He might 'proffer a knobbly allsort' (see *Infronophilia*) to his boss, by placing the story in a diary column or, worst case scenario, by having a pop jingle made up which sang both the salaries in full. In the family scenario, when Brunei are at home to Bangladesh, opulophiliacs might discuss exotic foreign holidays, as well as the possibility that one 'has one's eye on a new motor'. In extreme circumstances, mortgages might be revealed and interest rates exchanged.

[opulentiae, riches]

§

Parsciophilia: delight in the part-revelation of information.

One usually finds that parsciophiliacs are either parents or middle managers. Or both. Parents often find 'Husserl's Halt' (the sociologist's term for the manoeuvre of simply stopping dead in a conversation and refusing to continue) to be not only one of the most effective ways of diverting a child's attention from a sticky subject but also one of the most pleasurable. Indeed, perhaps there is some comparison to be drawn with middle managers; their delight, however, comes from the very *evident* abuse of power. They desire that their subjects know they are privy to more information, so they reveal part of it. Their version of Husserl's Halt is deliberately pensive and faltering. 'Of course, after September and the *new* set up, who knows about the Edinburgh office... I should... maybe... can I? ... no, I'd better not!' Exquisite. Their delight in a seven-second sentence leaves their victim with a seeming life sentence of unanswered questions. Sir Francis Bacon, who coined the phrase 'For also knowledge itself is power,' in his 1597 *Meditationes Sacrae* (a treatise on the ways to harness nature) found his follow-up book, *Meditationes Insurans* (a treatise on the ways to organise an insurance broker's head office) largely ignored when it posited 'He readily annoys he who tells only a portion of the story. Truly, it doth beautifully piss off thy minions'.

[pars, part; scientia, knowledge]

ζ

Parvanglophilia: delight in refusing to learn a language.

The derivation of this name is obvious, yet if you are in the presence of parvanglophiliacs, they surely won't understand. They are little Englanders *par excellence.* They have had ample opportunity to learn a language (sometimes the language of a place to which they return year after year) but they joyfully choose not to. When confronted with non-comprehension, they will turn to their party and give them that look which seems to say: 'See, poor blighter simply can't understand me! Crying shame for the chap!' They display a genuine sorrow that, yet again, the savage in front of them has failed to grasp the Queen's English, whether it be at the first service station outside Calais or at dinner in their old people's home, where Paulina, their nurse, doesn't know much of the language.

[parvum, little; anglia, England]

Pennaeophilia: delight in misleading a 'friend' regarding dress code.

More often than not this is a workplace pleasure. True, it might be fun to tell Barney to turn up to the golf club dinner in his jeans and t-shirt, but he's never going to do it. For maximum effect, a pennaeophile will hold on to the invitation for an event 'because you know you'll only go and lose yours if I give it to you'. In this way, they have managed to conceal the dress code 'Black Tie' from their office colleague (usually an underling whom they love to belittle). Thus the retro, brown checked suit sported by the poor unfortunate makes them look a little like a character in the Christmas episode of *Only Fools and Horses*. It is often worse if the pennaeophiliac manages to convince their colleague that a lunchtime event is black tie when it is actually 'Smart Casual'. If this is a media event, then, while all around them are in black shirts, black ties and black suits, they are bedecked in, cummerbund and dicky bow. It's as if Paul Daniels has walked into an Oswald Mosley rally. The pennaeophiliac is easy to spot. He is on the floor, in a pool of his own urine and hasn't stopped laughing all night.

[pennae, plumage]

Peregrinophilia: delight in using phrases in a foreign language.

Peregrinophiliacs delight in the use of numerous foreign words or phrases where one simple English one would suffice. The delight lies in the apparent air of sophistication gained from such usage, although timing has to be thought about: arguing that someone might be *petitio principii* while, say, celebrating a rugby league win in a communal bath might be hard to pull off. The ultimate trump card of the peregrinophiliac is the *noblesse oblige* card: pulling this out of the hat at a time least expected is a cure-all, 'get-out-of-jail-free' quote which excuses the bearer with an all-encompassing answer: sorry, but it's my family heritage that makes me such a cock. Ultimately, a peregrinophiliac loves to show depth where they feel you might be shallow. So, sometimes, when they say '*honi soit qui mal y pense!*' it is because they love the ebb and flow of the lyrical French language, yes. It is uttered, too, however, because it sounds so much better that 'Ner nicky ner-ner!'

[peregrinus, foreign]

§

Pertinophilia: delight in sitting on the outer seat on a train.

A luxurious commuter pleasure which has the potential to be enjoyed by everyone but especially immotophiles (qv). The daily standard is principally appreciated by those who are prepared to stand in a cluster at the point where their train doors will arrive for the full waiting time. For those whose trains leave every 30 minutes, this means being willing to endure a heroic 29 minutes of cluster time. Once aboard their Carriage (note the capital: this is more than a train to these people) they will take possession of the outer seat. This is their daily reward, their birthright, and shall not be given up without, if not a fight, then at least a jolly weak excuse. Several scenarios might ensue from the pertinophile's pursuit of pleasure. The most common retort is the Harrumphing Clump-past manoeuvre. This is a brusque, brushing movement that the later passenger must use to reach the inner seat. Any pain endured during this brush-past is viewed as mere penance by the pertinophile.

The 'Century of Cinema' is a trickier, more cunning gambit altogether, favoured by personal financial advisors, football referees and Virgos. This is the step by which one asks after the free, inner seat and motions as if to move into it, thus forcing the pertinophile to adopt the pose seen in cinemas when someone is coming through a row: that of the knees fully bent to one side. Then, the latecomer spends an age arranging their things, folding their coat into shop-state perfection, positioning their case, and generally keeping the pertinophile waiting. If done correctly, this can lead to a state of affairs where it is sometimes impossible to tell just who is enjoying themselves the most.

Finally, and most controversially, you can force the pertinophile to produce their excuse or argument.

Here, the latecomer might ask to occupy the outer seat. The pertinophile will then conjure up his excuse: long legs, need to be near a loo, phobia of train windows, that sort of thing. If this is not accepted, it may take the full argument to see the pertinophile back in a position of enjoyment.

A tiny, exquisite variant on the same pleasure is *Pertinophilia saccia*, in which the sufferer not only refuses to occupy the inner seat but also places their bag on it, maintaining its position despite grumpy motions from timid passengers. Some especially brave pertinophiles will even extend this pleasure to a full train with standing room only, feigning a foreign accent in order to hold on to the bag seat. Genius.

[pertinax, obstinate; saccus, bag]

§

Petrusophilia: delight in namedropping.

Namedropping is not so much a pleasure, more an ambrosial ecstasy. If practised properly, it can beat Nestle's Condensed Milk as a guilty pleasure. There is only one rule of *Petrusophilia*: never drop both names unless you absolutely have to. Always be on first name terms. It usually works. If it doesn't, and the 'Al' with whom you were discussing trade deficits is not identified, don't panic. Simply wait, and drop 'Al' once more, but perhaps add a little more situational detail, in order that his second name might be guessed.* For example: 'Absolutely, that's what Al thinks too. His last movie was affected so much by exchange rates, it was nearly cancelled'. See? Quite clearly Al Pacino, as any fule kno. Job done, and the realisation that you were talking about him all along and haven't yet been seen to officially namedrop *with both names* can only add to the pleasure.

If your bomb fails to hit its target even on the second pass, you might want to try steering the conversation round to a situation whereby you know your spouse will prompt you, thereby namedropping on your behalf (NB: a spouse's proxy name-drop can be both names). So, take this situation from *Depratts Book of Nominal Gravity*, for example:

Host: How is the venison, by the way? I picked it up in Borough Market, after I'd come back from that awards lunch.

Host's spouse: Oh, yes. Rupert had Stephen Fry doorstep him, didn't you darling?

Guests en masse: REALLY!

Host: Darling, I don't think Stephen was doorstepping me. [Note the single name still. And faux modesty.]

Host's spouse: Didn't he tap you on the shoulder and say, 'Well, hello, stranger!'

And so on. In this way, the petrusophile maintains his sense of superiority and need not even relate the denouement of the story, in which Stephen Fry did indeed say 'Well, hello, stranger!', only to find that it was, indeed, a stranger and go on his way having apologised for mistakenly disturbing our host. Sheer nectar.

Incidentally, petrusophilia takes its name from its patron saint, Peter, who, following the Transfiguration was said to be the biggest namedropper in the business. Jesus this, Jesus that. Must have been insufferable.

* This is thought to be the origin of the phrase 'second guessing'.

[petrus, rock]

§

Picfundophilia: delight in fooling celebrities or politicians into a dodgy photo opportunity.

Strictly speaking, even though we all (99.9 per cent at least) adore this philia, we are only picfundophiliacs by proxy. The true picfundophiliacs – a more or less literal translation being 'delight in the picture to make an arse of' – are the valiant troopers of the Press Photographic Corps. These brave men, whose everyday work is often dismissed by the use of the word *papparazzi*, soldier on bravely, putting up with the company of politicians, day in, day out, in the faint hope of finding them in a situation that will make them look like an arse. These are the heroes who, yes, admittedly brought you Lady Di in a see-through dress, but also, one day, might bring you Our Beloved PM next to a Cockburn's Port sign with the 'burn obscured.

Say no more.

[pictura, picture; fundus, bottom]

Plexisophilia: delight in buying the cheapest item.

This philia first saw the light of day in Victorian times. Indeed, there is an accompanying legend which holds that it was Queen Victoria herself who first began to practise *Plexisophilia*. Not content with the ruse of disguising herself as one of her subjects and venturing out of the palace to observe real life, she is said to have taken the whole thing one step further by entering early department stores. Never one to carry much money, she asked for the cheapest item in the store, which she duly bought before leaving. Her disguises were reported to have been pitiful (one was a small black kerchief which she wore over her crown) and most folk duly knew exactly who it was who they had served. Today, the staff of Harrods or Selfridges are themselves not amused when they are asked for the cheapest item in the shop by tourists brandishing £50 notes in one hand and a small 'bag for life' in the other.

[mulitplex, composite; saccus, bag]

Pluviapompophilia: delight in displaying cynicism to gung-ho new employees.

> Don't tell me not to live....! Don't tell me not to fly.... !
> Don't... rain on my parade!*

Were Bob Merrill and Jule Styne ever exposed to *Pluviapompophilia*? Whether they were or not, as composers of the above song they have become the talisman for a whole generation of rebels, eager to free themselves from the malevolent vibes of the pluviapompophiles. Studies have shown that pluviapompophiles are almost always simultaneously alavellophiliacs too (qv) or, if not, soon will be. Pluviapompophiles are not unlike vampires in their habits. They see the new intake as 'fresh meat', fine new lambs to the slaughter. It makes them smirk a little to see an array of newly suited and booted employees who still 'buy it'. It will make them smile beyond belief, though, to put these virgin soldiers right on so many points. Don't they realise, they theorise, that I have been here for forty years and it has never happened for me yet? (Let's not get into the chicken nor the eggs of this hypothesis.)

Most pluviapompophiles tend to occupy the position of 'veteran' in the office, and no doubt have some acute office nickname, unbeknownst to them. Some colleagues call them Dr No, for example, a fact which is little to do with their predilection for Bond and more to do with the fact that they never seem to say yes to anything.

'Is it sad that I can still hum the tune to this?

[pluvia, rain; pompa, parade]

Postlabophilia: delight in leaving a bugger's muddle when you resign.

Let's face it: unless you are particularly high up the company food chain – and by that I mean that the free health care or the share options have kicked in – the relationship between employer and employee these days is one of polite restraint at best and implicit hostility at worst. He who laughs last, laughs longest, and no one laughs quite so much as a postlabophiliac. These are the divinely lucky people who have 'done a runner' (office parlance). They have sought and found alternative employment and are now delighting in their so called 'handover' period. This is the period in which they give their successor or, better still, their temporary successor, enough insight into their job to convince them they are being told everything while at the same time concealing a whole bunch of facts and the *modus operandi* to actually get the job done. The tools of the trade of the postlabophiliac are 1) badly written bullet-point notes, 2) a 'don't say if they don't ask' policy and 3) a mantra of 'I'll make sure you get that before I go'. They adore the fact that the company made their working life hell by a sort of 'death by a thousand job cuts' around them but singularly failed to get them. Not to be confused with those people who accidentally leave behind a bugger's muddle. These people are known by the term 'useless gits'.

[post, after; labor, work]

Potestaphilia: delight in flicking channels.

This is one of the root philias in the entire *Schadenfreude* world, and thought to be the modern version of one of the potential triggers for dictatorship. Such a seemingly inconsequential delight, it can trace its roots back to the twelve Olympians and their desire to change the world below them by the mere flicking of a thunderbolt. This modern version is still all about control. OK, control and snoring. Think of it in the same way as a driver and a passenger. On a twisting, turning road, the driver is in no way so perturbed as the passenger, for the driver knows what the car is about to do as they are driving. So the Keeper of the Buttons is similarly at an advantage. They are pressing the buttons and relishing your increasing agony as it drives you to the borders of insanity. If only they resembled anything like the Olympians themselves: for a chiselled jawbone or a toned chest and six-pack might make up for such an annoying habit. Alas the nearest they come to ambrosia is the custard stain on their crotch.

[potestas, power]

ʓ

Precognophilia: delight in talking along with the words in a famous movie.

There is an old joke about two chaps watching a John Wayne movie. One, who has seen the movie before, bets the other that Wayne will fall off his horse when it gets to the top of the hill. The other duly takes the bet and loses, whereupon the first chap admits he has seen the film before and refuses to take the money. 'No,' says the second chap, 'I've seen it before, too, I just didn't think he'd be quite so stupid second time round!' Chap number one in this scenario may well have been a precognophiliac, someone who enjoys their own knowledge of a film or a song, regardless of the potential disadvantage to others.

Precognophiles are often fans of musicals, a genre with an inbuilt realm of disassociative reality which fosters a level of knowledge bordering on the bizarre. Specific films attract precognophiliacs, such as *Withnail and I*, *The Shawshank Redemption* and *An Affair to Remember*. Note also: *Preprecognophilia* is a specific, slightly darker strain in which the practitioner recites the offending lines a few seconds prior to their appearance, thus mimicking the effects of both a satellite link with digital delay *and* an annoying git. I believe in France it is legal to shoot these people.[*]

[*]You may need to check this.

[pre, before; cognoscere, to know]

ॐ

Presientophilia: delight in revealing prior knowledge.

As a child I genuinely believed that hunting around the house in the days leading up to 25th December, in search of your presents, was something which only went on in the *Beano*. Yes, I was vaguely interested in what might lie ahead, of course, but the sheer ecstasy of Christmas morning was one I would not have spoilt for the world. If, however, you *are* a 'shaker", then not only will you be bemused by my confession but, possibly, you might also be a presientophile. *Presientophilia* is the delight in displaying prior knowledge. This does not mean simply knowing the time of a departing train or the price of eggs at the greengrocer's: *Presientophilia* is a whole different card game. I say card game because you often find bridge players make the most accomplished presientophiles, it being a dark delight that should be ever so properly finessed.

Subtlety is of the highest importance here; *Presientophilia* is a dish best served almost in secret – it is the sixpence buried in the pudding. Privileged, sometimes secret information should be revealed with temperance, incurring a positively tangible quiver for its selected audience. It can be the news of an appointment which, once public, the presientophile lets slip they were told 'when they came round to ours for supper' (a good presientophile always 'lets slip' – they never blurt). It might be a pregnancy which you 'happen to mention' you were privy to, thereby making clear the extent to which your friendship with the subject exceeds theirs. ('They were only telling family and close friends at that stage'; are there any crueller words in the *Schadenfreude* phrasebook?) Or, sometimes worse still, it could be a statement of intent on a friend's behalf ('I understand they're going to be in Kenya in summer …') which leaves your audience bewildered, somewhat crestfallen and stammering 'Really… are you sure? They hadn't mentioned it'.

A true grand-master in this sombre art will even leave a delayed bomb, hardly signalled at the time, which goes off later, dawning on its victim some moments, even hours, after. Such a dark lord is of the highest order, should be respected, and may even wear a flowing black cape. It should be noted that politics breeds a large number of presientophiles; there is, perhaps, something untoward about a profession which can use the daily mantra 'I am *minded* to …' to mean 'A committee decided some time ago, and I will reveal soon'. Furthermore, the *modus operandi* of politicians in government, and the sheer amount of information they are unable to divulge, tends to require rampant *Presientophilia*, particularly in relations with their shadow colleagues.

The patron saint of presientophiles is Wikileaks founder Saint Julian of Assange.

* shaker; one who shakes wrapped presents to determine their nature
[pre, before; scientia, knowledge]

Priotiophilia: delight in the overtly trail-blazing holiday.

Essentially a sub-strain of *Supervillophilia* (qv) whereby the subject delights in being the first person they know to visit a certain destination.

So, here, the holiday becomes not a means for recuperation or sightseeing but a mere commodity. In an age where even your teenage son is doing a sponsored parasail over Antarctica, and with creeping urbanisation and the Global McVillage, sociologists believe priotiophliacs will have all but died out in twenty years. But then, hopefully, so will sociologists.

[primo, first; otium, holiday]

§

Priplaudophilia: delight in clapping first at the opera.

The first opera was written by a chap called Iacopo Peri, who is said to have almost stumbled upon this fresh musical medium while trying to resurrect Greek drama. In a world where, today, one might try to cure heart disease but end up inadvertently giving many an ageing letch a splendid erection, perhaps it is best to think of opera, then, as musical Viagra: a stiff by-product of a mistaken quest. Not long after the Peri original, there came, no doubt, the very first priplaudophile. Priplaudophilia is practised by estate agents, corporate lawyers and former war criminals – the same collective breed who demonstrate their painful knowledge of Italian when choosing the correct form of 'bravo' to cry, too. (Ever wondered why the ill-dressed chap next to you is always glowering? Yes, it's because you shouted 'bravo' when it should have been 'bravi': I mean, for heaven's sake, there's a quintet of them up there, man!) Rather than the exquisite golden silence favoured by the conductor, the orchestra and the singers at the end of the opera, the priplaudophile thinks it best you hear his clapping – before the last note has even reached the front row. It's not simply that he wants you to know that he considered the performance *great*. It's also that he wants you to know that *he knows* the performance is over. (If it's a Birtwistle opera, that's no mean feat, admittedly.) Not know where the end is? Not bloody likely. He's been studying the score and the recording (vinyl, naturally) for the last twenty years.

[primus, first; plaudere, clap]

§

Redeophilia: delight in returning unwanted gifts.

Redeophiles come in two similar but distinct varieties. *Redeophilia vulgare*, as its name suggests, is the most common and, to be fair, the most socially acceptable. It's a very personal philia in which at the very moment of taking receipt of a gift, the sufferer is visited by thoughts of how they will be changing it for something *not* wholly inappropriate and if it be clothes, exchanging them for something they might actually wear. *Redeophilia rara*, on the other hand, is a particularly acute form (often seen in friends and relatives of maldonophiliacs, qv, but not exclusively) which has to be witnessed to be believed. In this instance, a *rara* redeophiliac will receive the gift and instantly be informed that 'I have the receipt, if you want to change it.' As we know, the only answer to this charitable offer is a simple 'No! I love it' with as much conviction as can be mustered without attracting raised eyebrows. *Rara* sufferers, however, enjoy this knife-twisting moment a little too much and might reply 'Oh, yes, that would be great thanks. I probably will exchange it.' Believe me. I've seen it happen. It's not nice.

[redeo, return; vulgatus, common; rarus, rare]

ƻ

Rictusophilia: delight in smiling during an argument.

Rictusophiles know what they are doing. They *know* the destructive power of appearing to look like Jack Nicholson's Joker while you do your best to counter their hypothesis. They simply cannot help themselves. And herein lies the nub, so to speak. Much like their 'victory phrases'" (arguably the most annoying of which is the line 'Which merely brings me back to my original point!' inserted at the end of every opposing argument), the Cheshire cat smiles are sometimes quite simply addictive to the rictusophile. For these creatures, there is the accompanying feeling of danger: it feels intrepid, nerve-wracking even, to believe that they are being *so* annoying that at any moment, their opponent could lose patience and punch their lights out.

* A victory phrase is like an argument mantra, repeated regardless of logic, in an attempt to demoralise. Quoted from essay *Stuff Jeremy Bentham! The Pleasures of Mangled Morals and Lost Legislation*. Author, Ira Thumoeil. Self-published.

[rictum, with gaping jaw]

ς

Roginfanophilia: delight in quizzing your children's friends.

Again, a potentially misleading definition when summarised as above. In full, it should read: delight in quizzing your children's friends about their parents. Very often, a roginfanophile will tell you that their delight started absolutely honestly, with a genuine question of interest as they were making fish fingers and curly fries for their son and his friend. It might have been 'So, did you have a nice holiday, Jake? It was only when little Jake offered a glimmer of potential dirt ('…and we went to the beach. After mum and dad had finished arguing, we got ice creams') that they dared dip a tiny toe over the slidy slope to shameful sin. 'Really, arguing about what Jake?' That was years ago. Now, its not a tiny toe. Now they are positively body-boarding down the sleazy slope, screaming with exhilaration as they go. No sooner has Jake put down his school bag than they've got him pinned against the wall, angle-poise shining in his squinting eyes. 'Hey, Jake. Good day at school? Are your folks still not talking to each other because of how your dad looks at Peter's mum? Really? Did she? The whole bottle! In one night. Tell me, has she ever rung up those financial adverts you get during your kids' programmes? She *has*!' Heavenly.

[rogare, to ask; infans, child]

§

Ruberinophilia: delight in embarrassing the children.

Ruberinophilia is mainly a parental philia, although some uncles do occasionally show signs. It afflicts parents from the ages of first word to around 12 or 13. In this period, the parent (usually the father) will indulge in mildly or extremely embarrassing behaviour for their own pleasure, safe in the knowledge that it will do no lasting harm. This is occasionally referred to as *Ruberinophilia simpla*. After this age, all traces of *Ruberinophilia* are frowned on, particularly by the spouse, who fears that such conduct will result in the now obnoxious and hair-trigger tempered cro-magnon leaving the fold. Once all danger of this is past, anywhere between the ages of 18 and 25, serious *Ruberinophilia* can begin again in earnest. Practices then range from a little light 'dad dancing', through to 'worrying conversations with friends' ('So, Gareth, Helen tells me he met you in accident and emergency? Did I ever tell you about my time in hospital?') The umbrella term for the late-onset embarrassments is *Ruberinophila pater*.

[ruber, red; infans, child]

§

Ruinophilia: delight in witnessing another's downfall.

Just as the agony and the ecstasy that is Beethoven's Ninth Symphony opens up into its final race to home, there is a superb moment when a soloist declaims '*Freude!*' and the massed choir behind him echo it to spine tingling effect. Despite it being one of the most emotional moments in all music, a ruinophile will always, in their heads, replace the soloist's cry of '*Freude*' with the word '*Schade*', so tweaking to even greater perfection this most sublime of moments. At least as far as they are concerned. And so we come to the heart of this book. The definition that could simply read, effectively, '*Schadenfreude*'. For a ruinophille delights in the downfall of others – *Schade*, harm: *Freude*, joy. It is the finest strain; the purest form of any black delight; the original and the best.

Addendum: at time of going to press, genome experts from Cambridge University, working with psychologists in the City of Westminster, claim to have isolated the gene responsible for a more recent strain of *Ruinophilia*, namely *Ruinophilia res publica*. Although work is still in its early stages, it is thought this delight, the delight in the downfall of a politician, is both more satisfying and more prevalent than previously thought. Originally, it was envisaged it affected only 99 per cent of the population, but this appears to be moving upwards.

[ruina, downfall; res publica, politics]

Salmophilia: delight in wearing
loud clothes as a privilege of age.

First of all, one thing to clear up. There are two different types of older person who wear loud clothes. The first are those who knowingly do it as a statement of not just their age but their accompanying abandonment of respect for social expectations. The second are those who are significantly less knowing and have no such social agenda. This second lot fall more into the 'nature has found a way of telling us to beware' category, particularly if accompanied by an outsize Bay City Rollers pin-badge (in the form of a rosette) and a permanent smile. Genuine salmophiles conduct their day-to-day affairs as if living in a Jenny Joseph poem. They get their name from the salmon-coloured corduroys, which are often the first delight enjoyed and one that will stay with them when their bright-checked jacket is long gone. It is also worth making a note of arenas of engagement, which matter greatly to most salmophiles. Frequently, one will see them at classical concerts, for example, wearing vivid purple culottes. Good work.

Harder environments are the Opera House and a day at the races, where their good work in wearing loud clothing would simply go unnoticed amidst all the flamboyance. Rugby grounds work well and one can see a preponderance of folk in all manner of howlers. (Sorry – in all manner of age-appropriate clothing.) Football grounds, however, are to be avoided, as they are an environment where *Salmophilia* is simply not understood. Only attempt it if you are there because Beachy Head is busy.

[salmo, salmon]

§

Secringeniophilia: delight in revealing a previously unknown talent at a crucially relevant time.

A recent survey, conducted among the readers of *SMUG* magazine*, revealed that a staggering 88 per cent aspired to *Secringeniophilia* over all others. Secringeniophiles themselves say it is the 'pure joy' of the moment that delights, with the phrase 'wiping the smile off their face' featuring heavily in testimonials. By far the favourite arena for gratification is the workplace, revealing the talent in front of the boss in order to both confound and confute. If possible, the presence of the boss's boss turns pleasure into ecstasy. At home, *Secringeniophilia* can often have a lighter side which is best not discussed. Darker aspects include a secret talent revealed to show up a love rival. Also for home delectation is *Secringeniophilia vicenia*, one displayed in front of the neighbours. Again, *SMUG* subscribers' own true stories have shown an exotic mixture of talents thus revealed, from an overnight topiarist's spectacle to the chap who was pleased, to say the least, to have Andy Murray drop him off from his 'tennis knockabout with a mate' shouting 'You won't win next time, you old dog!' Another favoured arena for *Secringeniophilia* is the dinner party, usually the point at which the party retires to the drawing room, generally with the words '… and Bob is going to keep you all entertained while I make Irish coffees. I expect you were wondering what that set of knives and sheet of chipboard was for.'

Schadenfreude Macht Uber-Gemütlich – the international magazine of Schadenfreudians everywhere, and the only one now since *Schadenfreudian Slip* went bust, as *SMUG* delightedly reported in their March 1992 cover special. Their annual festival and conference, The Ugly *SMUG* Ball, is every August in Berlin. Entertainment is never pre-arranged (secringeniophiles turn up on the night) although the last night film is always the same: the secringeniophiliac's favourite, *Groundhog Day*.

[secretus, secret; inegenium, talent; vicinius, neighbour]

ʒ

Secroculophilia: delight in wearing sunglasses at inappropriate moments.

One of the few philias which is split 50-50 between males and females, the delights here are both practical and quasi-spiritual. 'If the eyes are the window of the soul, then we choose to put up the shutters' according to one sociologist. So true, and for so many reasons. Chiefly, it is in order to assist our raging *Vecolophilia* (qv). With the eyeline obscured, anything is possible. Having said that, a true vecolophile would not need to mask his gaze. Others insist that they gain their pleasure solely from the added mystery that the shades confer. Finally, there are those who simply can't help themselves. Here, if the eyes are the windows of the soul, it appears they should be boarded up with plywood and the police informed. Clearly, these are people who know the Hadean origins of the word 'shades' and who are more *secretus oculus* addicts rather than secroculophiles: some have been known to conduct their entire life in shades, even indoors, even in winter, thus rendering their lives something like a scene from an 1850s northern mill town in December.

[secretus, secret; oculus, eyes]

ʒ

Sedesophilia: delight in fixing a seating arrangement for maximum discomfort.

If you translated this philia and asked someone to guess what a 'chair lover' might like, the answers would take you far off the beaten track. Sedesophiles love using chairs as pawns, yes, but it is of course those chairs' occupants which are their currency. *Sedesophilia domus* affects the hosts of dinner parties, who take the time to make arts and crafts name cards to indulge their range of ultimately harmless, non-life-threatening vices: they might enjoy seating someone for matchmaking purposes for example, or seating someone to 'absorb' Norman and limit the damage of his only conversation, the one about the research he's doing into glass recycling.

All the more serious, and ten shades darker, is *Sedesophilia labora*, which is practised by middle managers and personal assistants up and down the land. The practitioner delights in using the seating plan as an instrument of torture. There's the Neck Twist, in which he seats you with your back to the action – at a work awards evening, for example – forcing you to crane your neck all night (you can opt not to turn round, but then end up staring into his smiling face for hours). He might use the Pincer, in which he seats you between two total nightmares. There's the Earbasher, which is reserved for ageing staff who just want 'a nice night out' but are deliberately placed next to the boss; the Bargepole, which is the inverse for young, thrusting types, seated so far away that the boss can't even see them; and finally, the worst one: the Lion's Mouth and Seat. This is when the sedesophile places you next to The Client. Don't be fooled by the name: it is so called because you have to listen and kiss arse at the same time.

[sedes, chair/seat]

§

Sermophilia: delight in talking about someone.

I am pretty sure I remember once hearing that a first draft of the lyrics to the popular song and jazz standard 'Please Don't Talk About Me When I'm Gone' included the couplet:

> If you can't say anything nice, say something vile,
> You sweet-voiced, dark delightin' sermophile.

Had it survived in the finished song it would have been almost certainly the first recorded reference to

Sermophilia. Sermophiliacs are not lovers of the *fruits* of gossip (see *Sermunculophilia*) but more lovers of the nature of a dissecting conversation. In this sense, they are both like and unlike predatory animals: alike because they love the act of taking apart the subject – enjoying it as a social occasion, with a sense of collective involvement – and yet not, because they don't need to do it to survive. Very often, sermophiles do not themselves pass on any gossip as such, nor does their tongue lash anyone in particular. And yet they adore the scene, and their sometimes passive stance but active euphoria in it. 'Feed me!' they are shouting, like a mushroom, 'Feed me with *dirt*!'

[sermo, talk]

§

Sermunculophilia: delight in gossiping.

There's a saying among sermunculophiliacs: 'It's not the taking part that's important, it's the taking *apart*.' Indeed, here are those people whom you might have thought had been left out of the definition above. These are the people who are not so bothered about the occasion, or the *craic*, or the event, they just want the currency: just the facts, ma'am, just the bare facts. They bring them, they trade them, they *live* for them. These facts are *so* enjoyable they might burn the equivalent of a hole in their pockets* if they didn't share them. Here, the delight is in the stuff, the goods, the lowdown. Their reading material is the biography, the diary pages of the papers, a trashy magazine if they're feeling particularly dirty today. Indeed, they are the sort of people who commonly tell you of their 'guilty pleasures' – anything from *OK!*, through *The Osbournes*, to *The Sun*'s 3a.m. Girls – to the point where you begin to realise that they don't have any innocent pleasures.

Not to be confused with *Sermophilia* (qv).

* A hole in their brain?

[sermunculo, gossip]

ဒ

Serusophilia: delight in driving down the outside and nipping in at the last minute.

Most of us have experienced serusophiles in one way or another. Some of us see them and hate them. Some of us see them and ignore them. Most of us, of course, *are* them. Come on! We've all done it, let's not pretend we haven't. Whether one lays claim to 'finding oneself in the wrong lane, a little late' or whether you admit that you were wilfully and blatantly trying it on is a matter between you and your god. But it can be delicious, can't it? Sailing down that soon-to-disappear lane. Eight hundred metres, keep going. Six hundred metres, keep going. Four hundred, two hundred – *keep going*! Then simply lean in, relying on the fact that you are driving a beaten up Suzuki Ignis to ensure the shiny Mercedes Benz driver lets you straight in. Wouldn't want to try it the other way round, though.

[serus, late]

ဒ

Sinophilia: delight in letting one go and not owning up.

Depending on which examining board they follow, students of Latin, brought up on Caecilius and Quintus, often don't get round to studying Plutarch's 'Boring Daily Lives of the Great Leaders'.* If they did, they would know that the famous cry of '*Et tu, Brute?*' not only had a follow-up (see *Eboracophilia*) but was in fact the second occasion on which Caesar had uttered this line. Indeed, many think that he was deliberately quoting himself, as a last dig at his former friend. The first occasion had been when Caesar had discovered that Brutus was one of the earliest known sinophiliacs, unmasked by Caesar himself by means of both a process of elimination and a truly sensitive Roman nose. Some say Brutus never forgave his emperor for revealing him as the origin of the *muta sed morta* and this was the final spur to join the band of imperial killers. (Brutus's reply on that first occasion, sadly, is much less quoted: 'No, I always own up to mine!')

These days, *Sinophilia* is a risky business, and one which can, no pun intended, backfire. Often, beginner sinophiliacs are easy to spot from their tendency to overact their disgust. Seasoned practitioners, however, tend to simply root themselves to the spot and smile. Indeed, the early draft of William Henry Davies' 'Leisure', only revealed on his death in 1940 has been adopted by some as their family motto:

'What is this life, oh sinophile,
If we've no time to stand and smile?'
Quite.

* *Boring Daily Lives of the Great Leaders*, Plutarch, PUP (Pompeii University Press). Includes a chapter on the afternoon naps of Romulus and Remus.

[sine, without; nomine, name; muta sed morta, silent but deadly]

Socrophilia: delight in calling people too early in the morning.

There is something almost pleasant about the old name for this philia – Mother-in-Law's Phone – that seems to put it in the same realms as Tennis Elbow or Housemaid's Knee. Indeed, many a squash game that has ended in a crushing defeat for one side sees them complaining of '…a touch of Mother-in-Law's phone this morning, hence… bit off my game'. It may sound like an excuse but it is serious. Why *does* a mother-in-law telephone at 8.30a.m. on a Saturday morning? Is it because, being of a certain age and having risen with the bakers (lunch by 7a.m.?), they are effectively feeling almost *post meridien* by 8.30 *ante meridien* and thus in need of a good natter? Such an interpretation is indeed charitable. The similarly timed call on a Sunday, however, comes with a hard-to-shake overtone implying that one is being positively ungodly in your slumber. Many a son-in-law, too, has been led to suspect that there is also a concurrent desire to interrupt the very best use of a morning glory. There is no empirical evidence to support this. Plenty of anecdotal evidence, however.

[socrus, mother-in-law]

Solopusophilia: delight in just doing one's job.

I remember fondly an episode of the old TV classic *Ripping Yarns* in which a family found their pedantic son *so* boring that they chose to speak in French, in order to avoid having to speak to him. No doubt, an early solopusophiliac. Another classic in the *Schadenfreude* catalogue, the definitive version of a strain of git we have known all our lives. These folk delight in the letter of the law. The spirit? Begone, ye vile beast. Solopusophiliac tendencies are often found running alongside an almost fundamental Christian view of the world ('No tattoos! No Beatles haircuts! Banned in Leviticus, you know!') they approach the minutiae of their daily drudge with sheer delight. And good luck to them. Often unfairly associated with the traffic warden community, today's practitioners are more likely to be found in politics, health and safety or the BBC contracts department.

[solo, only; opus, job]

ʓ

Somlocophilia: delight in sleeping where or when you should not.

Sleep crops up more than it probably should in this book. To anyone who has led a comfortable, nine-to-five existence, this might seem odd. To anyone who has had to endure some form of regular, work-induced sleep deprivation, it will not. Somlocophiles are probably from this latter category: less nine-to-fivers, more whenever-till-wheneverers. Saint Renaldo is the patron saint of 'extreme sleepers'. He is said to have been a worker involved in the roof of the Sistine Chapel – not the painting side, the tiling – who, because of Michelangelo's insistence on working until all hours, never found himself getting anywhere near his required eight hours. He was famous throughout all Italy for falling asleep at dinner parties, even the ones he himself was giving. He was martyred when he nodded off while cooking: he fell, face first, into a beef bourguignon, and still failed to wake up. He was stewed alive. With potato gratin and courgette batons in a white wine and fennel coulis served on the side. Ever since, the practice of 'extreme sleep' – in a shop, at the dinner party table, at a school parents' evening – has been carried out in his name. And it is delightful, isn't it?

[somnus, sleep; locus, place]

Sornaurophilia: delight in knocking up some quick pasta in return for a 'Gordon' or 'Nigella'.

The very phraseology of this philia's defininition owes much to the early 1990s when it became one of the much vaunted 'new philias', which many hoped would usher in a new age of social blackness and economic one-sidedness: 'A Fair Deal for Me, *Sorry* to See You're Screwed' was the hopeful rallying cry.

In actual fact, this philia goes all the way back to feudal times and was originally called Chicken Payback.[*] Back then, Baron One might treat Baron Two to a feast, the centrepiece of which was a 'bird within bird' roast – the woodcock, in a pigeon, in a chicken, in a turkey, right up to a horse. Possibly. When it came to the payback, Baron One would have to hide his disdain when a simple chicken was revealed. When the sornaurophile Baron Two cut into his meagre offering with an 'And guess what is inside?', he would delight in revealing: stuffing. The contemporary version is the same, in essence, and can be enjoyed safe in the knowledge that one's guests are effectively a captive audience. So, if you have been royally treated to a first-rate meal from the pages of Nigella's latest tome, you might enjoy returning the favour by explaining when it's your turn that you've 'gone for a retro theme' and thought it would be great 'to revisit chicken in a basket!'. A great modern twist on chicken payback.

[*] No reference to the great soul classic of the same name by The Bees

[sordes, dirt; non, not; aurum, gold]

Strictophilia: delight in drinking but leaving before your round.

One of the hardest philias to pull off with aplomb, this translates as simply delight in being tight. That is about the nub of it but, if executed correctly, a seasoned strictophile can leave others in a room not just unaware of their deception but somehow actually grateful for their faux generosity. They can often be spotted by their language, which will be peppered with phrases like 'Let me get this one', and 'OK, who wants another?' And yet, somehow, when they 'simply had to' leave, only then did it dawn that they had not actually bought a drink. Genius.

Tips for the perfect strictophile: case the joint, timing your arrival with someone else's bar visit. Monitor drink patterns and make your lavatory visits pay. And keep your wallet in a difficult to reach pocket/place, to buy yourself valuable removal time, allowing others to step in.

[strictus, tight]

§

Stultinfanophilia: delight in another parent's unachieving offspring.

Always more pleasurable when it turns up in what might be considered unexpected quarters, *Stultinfanophilia* is a dish best served almost imperceptibly. Unexpected might mean in the offspring of high-achieving parents, for example, or maybe, potentially more enjoyably, in the offspring of those higher up the payscale. How delicious it is to be at the boss's summer garden party – casually throwing into conversation how your son hasn't done too badly, although being Lucasian Professor of Cosmology does mean he doesn't ring home much – and then being able to throw comforting bones his way: 'Norman, the hospitality sector is growing massively and your son being a waiter, well, he's ideally placed at the heart of that!' Simply divine. Or perhaps 'Look, McDonalds are a *great* employer. And if he works his way up from drive-thru…'.

Remember, stultinfanophiles, do not overdo it. This is a finessed joy, almost the caviar of the *Schadenfreude* world. Savour the subtleties. So, at the CERN Four Year Anniversary Celebration: 'Professor, lovely to meet you. My daughter Emily was telling us she had met your Zac today. Professionally. Anyway, how is work?' Of course, Zac was in court, charged with desecrating a war memorial. And Emily sent him down.

Related philias include *Turparphilia* and (not to be confused with) *Callidinfanophilia* (qv both).

[stultus, thick; infans, chidl]

§

Stultosophilia: delight in high-lighting someone's mispronunciation.

So many infernal levels of delight exist within the realms of *Stultosophilia* that it caught the eye (or is it hand?) of Dante when he came to write his mighty tome. Found in the third level of hell in the first drafts, but sadly removed from the finished product by a lisping editor, was a reference to the Italian author's own love of a little stultosophilic delight. Today, most practitioners agree that the first pleasure is felt within, an internal chortle at the offending word. Let us say, for sake of argument, it is one of the many great composers who collectively draw together to make the world of classical music a minefield for those armed not with a postgraduate degree, years of research and a chair in musicology but merely their own lifetime of common sense. Delibes, step forward, perhaps. So, the stultosophile has his internal chortle when he hears the word 'DelEEbeez'.

Another person might feel they could die happy, but not the stultosophile. He might go for Level Two pleasure which means adding a smug 'Quite!' upon hearing. For Level Three he might manage to insert the word, correctly pronounced, in his next sentence. Level Four pleasure is out of the stultosophile's hands and would come only if their friend happened to say 'Oh, of course, Deleeb. Yes.'

Finally, if that milestone is not passed, they can, on rare occasions, hit a further one: the stultosophiliac's equivalent of the multiple orgasm. In this author's life, it has only happened once, on the occasion of his wedding, when the officiant saw the groom's middle name, Georges, as a curiously Cockney moniker which had perhaps lost its apostrophe rather than the gift of a French-loving father. With the nature of the setting, namely repeated vows, it resulted in a stultosophile's paradise, a sort of tennis match with the name pronounced incorrectly on one side then correctly on the other, over and over. Memorably divine.

[stultus, fool; os, mouth]

Suapecophilia: delight in another's precarious financial position.

This is a philia that has spread exponentially since what many still refer to as the '1929-style market crash', desperate not to say the 'D' word.[*] Now, with many folk in a far worse position than they were before, neighbour has smiled upon neighbour in that across-the-hedge, 'my lawnmower is sit-on and yours is virtually shears on a wheel', smug sort of way and rampant *Suapecophilia* has set in. For any semblance of enjoyment, it is important to note that the person one is 'feeling sorry for' does not actually reveal their financial position. This would be no fun. To have brusque Yorkshiremen wandering around, mouthing off about not having 'two *sous* to rub together' is simply spoiling the main joys of *Suapecophilia*. For it to truly work, one needs to be able to offer them a drink on the way home from work with the line, 'Don't worry, it's on me!'

[*] Indeed, some avoided the 'D' word so much that many are now confused as to what D it actually stood for. The serious money is on death, or destruction. There's some outside betting it could have been D for Greek crooner Demis Roussos, but I'm not so sure.

[sua, their; pecunia, money]

Supervillophilia: delight in an exotic holiday.

Many an infrenophiliac (qv) has found themselves opting out of their black delight purely to follow the 'one true path' of *Supervillophilia*. This seasonal pleasure comes with its own, inbuilt, trigger question which should act as a lighthouse to all around to keep them from floundering on the conversational rocks – 'Are you going anywhere nice this year?' If this question is uttered by anyone other than a hairdresser, then alarm bells should ring: this is a supervillophiliac at work, happy in the knowledge that should you return the question it would unleash tales of 'the little place they've discovered' which is 'just so unspoilt', etc. The full delight for a supervillophiliac comes from the most understated descriptions they can muster. So 'just going to nip off to a little hut we've found' may be Tuscany; 'it's not unlike Brighton' is how they describe St Petersburg; and 'oh, just a little spot off the coast of Ireland' – New York. This disarming downplaying is done solely for the sport of face-fooling, the subsidiary delight of seeing you raise your eyebrows when you work out that 'our little place in the country' means you have been talking to the Duke and Duchess of Devonshire.

[superbus, proud; villa, villa]

Tabidophilia: delight in passing on a cold.

Not to be confused with novaletudophiliacs (qv), who simply (simply?) delight in being ill. A tabidophiliac comes with an altogether more malevolent side.

These are the people who sit through 'Bring your Daughter to Work Day', not to mention 'Bring your Pet to Work Day', all the while wondering whether it would be a good time to suggest there be a 'Bring your Contagious Disease to Work Day', too, at some point. For that is their delight. It is something they do in the name of 'soldiering in to work', but most in the office know that, with only their infirm mother and repeats of *Terry and June* on ITV3, their life would be truly miserable were they to have stayed home. For not only do they rejoice in thinking about their bug going round ('Doctor says it's not contagious', they lie, not having visited) they positively deck the place with bunting when they hear someone utter those quasi-sexual words 'I got this from you, you know!' Result.

[tabidus, infectious]

⅊

Tarcelerphilia: delight in driving slowly in the fast lane.

It is far too simple to classify tarcelerphiliacs as simply 'sticklers' – or even 'caravan-towing '50s dropouts', as Jeremy Clarkson might say. They hold passionate views, yet come in two distinct flavours. Tarcelophilia prima sufferers are, to be fair, half delighting and half suffering. These are the types who are in a car that is way past its scrap-by date and, although they are smiling blandly like the baddie in *The French Connection* as you overtake them in the inside lane, you can rest safe in the knowledge that, at 70m.p.h. their car is shuddering wildly and they cannot hear the radio above the noise of the engine. Some wear ear defenders as standard. *Tarcelophilia secunda* types are more open to accusations of analism because they truly do believe they are fighting the good cause on Britain's roads. Despite the fact that the unofficial speed limit on Britain's roads appears to be 80m.p.h., they boldly fight the fight for the letter of the law. Indeed, this is where the dichotomy lies. Only yesterday they might have been observed doing the limit: it is only when all around them are speeding that they delight in going slower.

Standard symptoms include a shaking of the head in the mirror, complete with implied 'tut'. Other signs are a wagging finger (again, observed in the mirror) and the occasional one hand held aloft, to signify 'Look, what can I do. It's the law!' Seasoned tarcelophiles will even negate all their 'good' driving, asking passengers to take the wheel as they carefully flash ten fingers, seven times, in the mirror. Most are not deterred by a testy, 80-something speed past in the slow lane. An 80-something speed past in the slow lane, brandishing a baseball bat, with fingers pointed to and from the driver's eyes may, however, deter even hardened tarcelophiles. Bump them from behind with your tinted-windowed Hummer and you have probably cured them.

[tardus, slow; celeritas, speed]

Tecibophilia: delight in eating food you deliberately didn't order 'because you weren't hungry'.

Let's be honest here: this is largely a female delicacy. Tecibophiliacs are almost always women. Their delight is two-fold. Firstly there is the delight in woefully under-ordering food at restaurants, thus making them feel, if not necessarily look, like angelic figures. My word, aren't they being good, eating so healthily. Secondly – and this is by far the greater pleasure for most tecibophiliacs – there comes the order itself. At this point, they exercise Spouse's Rights to claim half (sometimes more) of their partner's food, usually the part consisting of potato-based products. In the name of 'just having one', they quite simply steal (for stealing it is in my book: and this *is* my book) the lion's share of your food. If you were to move your food aside, or even petition them to desist, then accusations of childishness and petulance will make sure that the tecibophile comes out on top.

Famous tecibophiliacs in history include Carl von Linde, who formulated his theory on refrigeration with reference to his personal pleasures. Like many teciboophiliacs after him, he had the habit of eating only half of his food, thereby always making himself feel good for not having munched the lot. Tecibophiliacs down the years have imitated this habit for their own sombre enchantment, leaving fridges everywhere with half-eaten comestible relics.

[te, you; cibus, meal]

Tefamaphilia: delight in witnessing a celebrity in an everyday pickle.

In these days of whatever the latest mnemonic is for the coalition government (personally I favour CoLiDe as a suitably 'car crash-friendly' axiom), I imagine I am not alone in thinking life is quite confusing enough, thank you very much. Former political adversaries now appear as if in a 'before' picture for a Channel 4 documentary on conjoined twin separation; more people listen to Chris Evans on the radio than voted for one of the parties in power; and a small child with a face like one of Barbara Cartland's poodles is dishing out the cash at the Treasury. Never mind explaining that to a resurgent coma victim, just try it on someone who dozed off for forty winks. Thankfully, though, there are some things, which not only help de-clutter the icon-filled desktop of our brains but also raise a *schadenfreudal* smile in the process. For those who were confused by the seeming abundance of people nicknamed Fergie in public life, along comes one of them, helpfully, to stir a small moment of *Tefamaphilia* within each and every one of us.

First of all, the two Fergies. One is a performer who travels the world, singing like a canary, wearing outrageously flamboyant clothing and generally courting publicity. The other is in the Black-Eyed Peas. When the former did her best to engage in a small spot of public disambiguation with her namesake by discussing her (royal) ex with a Sunday tabloid reporter, she was close to mapping out the boundaries of this philia. Strictly speaking, it was not actually a case of *Tefamaphilia* at work. *Tefamaphilia* is normally reserved for when we see celebrities in a more quotidian jam than this: receiving a parking ticket on their Maserati; being refused entry to a nightclub, while sporting the very latest designer line of '*Scis quis ego sum?*' T-shirts; and the *pièce de résistance*, being stopped for a search while going through customs ('Are these your wedges, Mr Cruise?').

[te, you; fama, famous]

§

Testudophilia: delight in walking slowly.

It would be interesting to organise a conference one day for testudophiliacs. Apart from seeing if they ever made it from seminar to seminar, it would simply be fascinating to see such a potentially disparate array of people in one once-passable, edge-of-town hotel at the same time. For testudophiliacs tend to be drawn from some rather distinct groups. Through the annoyingly slowly revolving door, which stops at intervals should it detect you are in a slight hurry, would come: lovers or the newly married; tourists; journalists doing the opening sentences of their item for the six o' clock news; cowboys (who will tell you that they are, strictly speaking, not testudophiliacs at all but simply practitioners of 'the art of mosey'); and, of course, zombies. These champions of the slow walk (a movement which, I think it's fair to say, sadly does not have the same sort of end-reward product as, say, the Slow Food movement) would do well not to share their hotel with a calxarophiliacs' (qv) conference otherwise they might well go home lame. I need not identify these people any more. You know who they are. Sadly, they don't. They are like lorries on the A1, oblivious to the plodding parade of cars left in their wake. Or are they?

[testudo, tortoise]

§

Tollophilia: delight in dumping someone.

Probably a specialised form of *Malnuntiophilia* (qv) this pleasure has increased exponentially with the growth in the availability of technology. There was a time, back in the days when women were women and men were gits, when one simply longed for the pleasure of looking someone in the whites of their eyes and saying 'It's not you, it's me'. The double pleasure, really, because not only had you gotten there first, but you had been able to say *La Ligne de La Plaquer** as the old French knights called it, namely: *Ce n'est pas vous, c'est moi*. Today, sadly, modern knights are not quite so gallant. Contemporary twists on the old joys include: a) setting the legend 'S'nt u, s'me' as their iPad screensaver before running; b) sending Stephen Fry a tweet that you are planning to dump someone, hoping he will retweet it; and c) the popular Drive-By Dumping, in which you simply open a tinted window, and throw a heavy object out, around which is wrapped the line 'X U, ✓ 3 I'.

Second Life dumping is also growing steadily, in which the pleasure-seeker kicks the person's avatar into touch. When the victim looks up from their computer, the dumper is gone.

* The Dumping Line

[tollere, to get rid of]

⌘

Tribuphilia: delight in being nominated.

Let me be perfectly clear: despite the etymology here, this is *not* a delight in winning awards. A tribuphile is a lover of the period of nomination, prior to an awards ceremony (presuming they have been nominated, that is). This period is *their time*. It is pure, unadulterated potential. They are a potential winner and, of course, others are not! It is better quality time than even the time after the announcements – even if they have won. For a tribuphile, having been nominated puts them in such a beautifully sweet position. In good company (usually, unless they are up for a People's Choice TV award) and with a spotlight shining smack in their face. Some of this does continue if they win but, in much the same way as the quality of sleep is never the same once you have risen from the sofa, the quality of the limelight, even post-win, has just a tinge of 'it's all in the past now' about it. It's as if the nomination period is akin to arousal and excitement, while the ceremony is the money shot, and boy does it make them feel dirty. Warning: if a tribuphiliac loses an award, a yoke of dirty clouds envelops their shoulders. It can be grim. Best keep away from the break-up tapes. Under no circumstance allow the sufferer access to 'Frank Sinatra sings for Only the Lonely'. It could prove fatal.

[tribuae, awards]

Tubaphilia: delight in farting while walking in headphones.

Does a phone ring in a locked room if there's nobody there to hear it? Probably. Can anyone hear your flatulence if you have your headphones turned up loud and you can't hear it yourself? Most definitely, but the tubaphile does not give a monkey's. This is one of those delights that never speaks its name in polite company, but too many of us have heard the evidence for it not to exist. The essence of this pleasure is in the uncertainty. The internal logic goes like this.

Fact 1: I just let one go.
Fact 2: On the train platform!
Fact 3: Mind you, I didn't hear it.
Thesis: Maybe nobody did.
Anti-thesis: Of course they did.
Conclusion: Ah, who cares?
Fact 4: Oops. Did it again.

[tuba, trumpet]

Tudolophilia: delight in not drinking.

As Latin scholars and over-passionate readers of Asterix may quickly realise, if one were to translate 'delight in not drinking' into the words of the ancient Romans, it would not come out as *Tudolophilia*. This is because almost the chief delight involved here is not the lack of drink but the subsequent opportunities it presents (qv *Ampropaschophilia*). Seasoned tudolophiles adore the practice of filling up other people's glasses while at best nursing or at worst abandoning their own. As a result, the moment they hear the first even partially slurred word arrive (and it comes surprisingly early) they begin to conversationally 'fish' with leading questions which they hope will encourage squiffy colleagues to share too much. The following conversations are then remembered word for word, ready for later embellishment. For the chief delight of *Tudolophilia* is time-delayed and, much like revenge, best enjoyed cold. The following morning, the tudolophile, who has a brain like a court stenographer, will use his detailed account as the basis of the post-mortem of the night before. They employ a live, speech version of Photoshop to embellish and airbrush the exploits of the previous evening, safe in the knowledge that no one can truly challenge their account.

[tu, you; dolus, trick]

Turpamicophilia: delight in hanging around with an unattractive friend.

If there is the perfect murder, then surely there can be the perfect philia? The philia that no one can ever pin on you. If so, then this is it. Yes, it so happens that my best friend is no work of art (unless you count the *Pile of Bricks*). And yes, it so happens that I was considered, by my schoolmates, 'Person Most Likely to Become a Film Star' in our leavers' book. (Indeed, I did appear on *Look East* when we started the 'Say No to the Chesil Road Recycling Centre Reduced Opening Hours' campaign: sadly, the campaign failed.) And indeed it is true that, for some reason her doctor can't establish, my friend does suffer from recurring nightmares in which she features as the 'before' picture to my 'after' in an advert for facial disfigurement. *But…* our friendship is entirely genuine and valid.

Yes, turpamicophiliacs *love* their dark pleasure, persuading their friend that they shouldn't go for that makeover and that they are perfect the way they are.

[turpis, ugly; amicus, friend]

ʮ

Turparphilia: delight in the less than pulchritudinous nature of a friend's offspring.

An important point to note at the start here is that most turparphiliacs are childless. In a small number of instances however, *Turparphilia* might also be displayed by members of those families whose every gene appears to be perfect – as if they had all been bred in futuristic experiments with the intention of one day appearing in American perfume advertisements. These are, it is fair to say, the hardest turparphiliacs to bear. Most of us, if confronted by a proud parent complete with new baby in tow, would, I dare say, simply opt for a platitude. 'Isn't she gorgeous', would perhaps suffice. 'Oh, how cute', maybe. Even, 'Aw, he's got his father's eyes'.

Turparphiliacs, however, will deliberately emphasise the baby's lack of beauty by praising an altogether irrelevant point. Think of the line in 'Don't put your daughter on the stage, Mrs Worthington', where Noël Coward writes 'She has nice… hands, to give the wretched girl her due' (Coward clearly a committed turparphiliac). So, in the baby department they might say, 'Oh, hasn't she got beautiful…feet', or even try a diversionary 'Oh, what a lovely cot!' Largely, it has to be said, the person doing this does so because they think it to be true. It is true, indeed – not all babies can be bonny. This much stands to reason. So, a turparphiliac might convince themselves that they are merely being honest. Of course, they are not. They are damning with faint praise. They are delighting in the fact that the doting couple appear to have brought forth a minger of the highest order.

If childless themselves, of course, they are tempting fate by doing so. If, however, they are the proud parent in one of those obnoxious, wholesome families who were all modelling at the age of ten and have names like Toby or India, then they can delight in your *good fortune* till the cows come home. And it appears one of them just has – only you wrapped it in swaddling clothes and laid it in a manger. In many well-to-do families, *Turparphilia* is often referred to by its more artistic sobriquet of 'praising Friedrich for his frame'. The phrase is said to come from 1830s Germany, when the romantic artist Caspar David Friedrich was at his height. His forward-thinking, often melancholic paintings, many showing a lonely figure in a vast romantic landscape, were sometimes met with less than outright praise. Hence, when his enemies wished to belittle his paintings, they would openly admire his frames rather than his canvasses.

[parva, young; turpa, ugly]

§

Uncidamnophilia: delight in losing weight.

See *Fustisophilia*.

[uncia, inch; damnum, loss]

§

Valephilia: delight in saying good-night to expose someone leaving early.

We've all done it at some time or other. You need to leave work either early or, in these macho 'What d'ya mean, you've got to leave before midnight?' times, maybe you simply want to leave on time. So you quietly prepare. You turn off your computer early. You have your bag 'left on reception' by a friend (nice touch) so that you can walk past the boss without it. You try to choose the moment: you have to let a couple of ideal times pass because they are simply too early. But there's never a right time. Even though you have your route planned down a different corridor, in the end you simply have to make a cool dash for it. This is when the valephiliac strikes. Blaring out around the office, as if it were on some sort of ethereal, fortissimo, airborne tannoy: 'B-Y-E, K-E-I-T-H!' It's like you are hearing it in slow motion. If he (and it is more often a he: short sleeved shirt, first moustache, perhaps born-again) is truly enjoying his delight, he might preface his cry with 'Oh, are you off? Right, well, then… B-Y-E K-E-I-T-H!' Everyone looks up. The boss looks up. The office pianist stops playing. And the valephiliac comes in his pants.

The inverse, enjoyed during a person's late arrival is often called *Salvephilia*.

[vale, farewell; salve, hello]

§

Vecolophilia: delight in being sexist.

This is just one of the sins of old age, so-called because they become more prevalent with maturity. The etymology of the name sheds useful light on its practitioners; these are the true colours on show here. Often given away by the use of the word 'filly' in polite conversation, vecolophiles are using their ageing years to forgive themselves sins which, previously, they might have covered up. In this instance, it is their inherent sexism. They see varying degrees of severity at work in all things. Of course sexism *per se* is not what is in play here. They are merely being *nostalgic* for the things that they were brought up on: long hot summers, knotted hankies, whelks, blatant racism and a rather outdated attitude towards women. What is so wrong with *Mind your Language* and *Benny Hill?* Surely it's just gentle fun!

Indeed, many vecolophiles meet every year at summer solstice in Teddington (Camp Bestial, est. 1992), not far from Teddington Lock. They make a pilgrimage to the plaque in the former Thames TV car park, then sit up all night, telling double entendre jokes and chanting the mantra ('what a lovely pair') before performing a filmed chase dressed as nuns and nurses. Later, as the sun rises over the Hogs Back (now re-christened Benny Hill), they watch the whole thing back on a large screen, specially speeded up, while musicians play cheesy sax tunes extra fast. Ah, the good old days.

[vero, true; color, colour; quam pulchra duo, what a lovely pair]

§

Verolatophilia: delight in being visibly on a train which someone misses.

The etymology behind this one is confusing and open to numerous interpretations. Due to the train-based nature of the philia, many have presumed that the 'right side' it refers to is somehow 'the tracks'. Others, and with possibly more academic weight on their side, posit that it is merely the window or the door that one is on the right side of (the fact that Roman chariots had no windows seems to pass them by). Regardless, this is a deep-seated philia, which its practitioners love partially for its feelings of power and partially due to the only very occasional nature of its arrival. It is a moment of true, old-fashioned *Schadenfreude*.

Comfortably seated – is there an element of *Immotophilia* (qv) about this? – and about to embark on one of life's other great pleasures, a journey, one has one's privileged position reinforced by the marvellous view of someone running for the train. You might see them simply run and fail and give them your best 'Oh, I say, hard luck, old chap' half frown. You might see them run, lunge and take a fall on their arse, thus increasing the pleasure tenfold. I truly hope that, one day, you will be fortunate enough to enjoy one moment of *Verolatophilia* enjoyed by the author, one day on the London Underground. It involved a chap running for the tube, and, in his blind panic lunging for the door, missing, falling flat on his face on the platform before standing up and, in a moment of caution, saying 'Ooh, is this the train for Wimbledon?', only for the tube door to close immediately on his foot. As he managed to pull it out with the train drawing away, the passenger to my left was heard to utter – 'Er, yes' – before cracking up.

[verus, correct; latus, side]

§

Verophilia: delight in being right.

See *Indiverophilia*.

[vero, truth]

§

Vestiophilia: delight in revealing that a celebrity has worn an outfit more than once.

It never fails to baffle me as to where vestiophiliacs find their joy. Does the entire world presume, as they seem to, that anyone deemed to be 'a celebrity' has somehow given up the right to wear clothes more than once? Are they meant to simply throw each outfit away, donate everything to charity or rent out their clothes? (Renting clothes: what a strange celeb-land concept, up there with pre-nuptial agreements, tit-tape and 'beards').[*] And yet, somehow, vestiophiles – almost always journalists – do relish their sartorial revelations, inevitably reaching for their excruciatingly bad headlines. 'Double J-lo-pardy!' 'Jennifer Againiston!' Yes, it's pain for us, but it is sheer pleasure for them. If only there were some god of print who could likewise expose the use of recycled headlines.

[*] That's *beards*, not beards.

[vestio, clothe]

§

Vetunectophilia: delight in one's school.

An old school tie is but a metre long, thinner at one end than the other and generally sports a pattern in

169

which a sane person would not be seen decomposing. Despite this, it is capable of casting shadows that run not in terms of furlongs and miles but in terms of years and centuries. Now not worn so often, it can still cast its shade – or, some might insist, its light – from its resting place in the wardrobe. The walk-in wardrobe, of course. What vetunectophiles cherish are those moments that give them superiority over unconfident colleagues. They know that a passing side-reference (ok, it was a clunky name-drop the size of a mountain boulder) to '... there was one time, when Uppingham decided it would put on some Shakespeare...' has probably made you stop time for a moment and think back to your alma mater. Not sure if we ever *did* Shakespeare at our comprehensive. Unless you count Lucy Shakespeare, in fifth form.

[nectare, to tie; vetus, old]

᛫

Vetuscholophilia: delight in checking people out.

A massive increase in the number of vetuscholophiliacs was witnessed in the late 1990s, which sociologists put down to both the backlash against the post-70s correctionalism and the appearance of 1990s anti-heroes. Despite the continued growth in vetuscholophile-style behaviour, there are still many people who simply use this as a cover for their rampant *Nonrenovophilia* (qv). At its most simple and best, though, *Vetuscholophilia*, in the proponent's mind, is not unlike the appreciation of great art. More often than not you will hear them, if discovered, talk of 'the view of Derwentwater' or some such divine landscape. For a vetuscholophile, a beautiful view is a beautiful view, whether it be stationary in Umbria and swathed in a fine mist and verdant woodlands, or in motion in Salford and clad in tight leggings and a sweater. They feel both are potential moments of delight, one of them adjudged by society to be darker than the other, yet both of which should be grab-able with the eyes.

[vetus, old; schola, school]

§

Viatorophilia: delight in relishing one's partner's 'innate sense of direction'.

This is a passion to be enjoyed on two very different levels. At one level, yes, there *are* those who delight in never having to open a map because their nearest and dearest does *genuinely*, 90 per cent of the time, have a wonderful, in-built sat nav, which seems to work with the precision of a computer. Of course, computers go wrong. The delight many might take in turning one's partner off and on again is neither likely nor lawful, so it is at this point that level two of *Viatorophilia* kicks in, namely the ironic level. This is far more enjoyable than level one and, like any good level, contains lots more things to see and do – previously unknown roads, which weren't available on level one; new areas of countryside; the same new areas of countryside, again, and so on. And, of course, levels of delightful semi-questions offered up like lobbed balls, for your partner to smash back down in anger. 'Are we actually meant to be driving *on* the the Cerne Abbas giant?' 'No, of course we're bloody not!' Pleasures like this only come round once a week at best, so best just keep quiet and enjoy.

[viator, passenger]

ဌ

Vidicophilia: delight in talking to people via their children.

Let's instantly clear something up: this does not involve the spirit world. No one is making contact with anyone from beyond the grave. Indeed, vidicophiles tend to believe themselves to be the most no-nonsense of people who, just from time to time, in order to make their point a little more forcefully, enjoy choosing a third party as the conduit for their views. It might be as harmless as something like 'My word look at your hair, Toby, it's so long' (translation: Son, get this boy's haircut, he looks like a hippie) but it could also be something more serious: 'Gosh, Jane you're home late tonight. And my, don't you look grown-up' (translation: What in God's name are you two doing letting her roam the streets till all hours? And dressed like a slut!). Sometimes, with age comes a more direct approach, when vidicophiliacs might simply enjoy pointing out the error of their children's parenting methods: 'Now, will you just look at little Ben, and his running around *unchecked* while his parents drink gin! Ah, bless him'. No translation necessary, perhaps. Interestingly, Herbert Marshall McLuhan, scholar and guru of the marketing men, is said to have been been very close to his grandmother, who by all accounts was one of the first vidicophiliacs to go public. His seminal marketing line, 'the medium is the message', is believed to have been something he carried with him since childhood, having been the medium through which his grandmother channelled her thoughts to his mum. (Again, just in case of confusion, *not* a spirit world thing.)

N.B. *Vidicophilia denuptia* is soon to be reclassified as a 'syndrome' not a philia, principally because, despite its darkness, when it strikes, no one, not even the subject, enjoys it one bit. V.D., as it will be called, occurs usually when a marriage has broken down and parents chose to communicate via third parties – not lawyers (yet) but their own children. 'Will you tell your father that if he insists on taking the car today then I won't be able to get the shopping in and therefore he won't have his favourite steak and chips waiting for him on the table when he gets home!'. 'And will you tell your mother that your father needs to get to a meeting on the other side of town so she will have to take the bus – that is if she can pull herself away from her Facebook friends!' If you don't know the sort of thing, then count yourself lucky.

[vicarius, proxy; dicere, to say]

ᛊ

Vigintiunophilia: delight in revealing someone's age.

There is still work to be done in dispelling the myth that this is a largely male philia, played out on paranoid females, desperate not to be written off as, heaven forbid, '*over thirty*'! Thanks to Bruce Forsyth's pioneering work, this philia can be enjoyed by both sexes. People do many things to hide their true age. In one example a TV presenter, in order to sidestep the vigintiunophiles around her, deliberately lied about her age with the same recurring number. Admirably, she let all around her know that she *was* 'lying' about her age, including the people she was 'lying' to; her justification was that the sad, twisted world of TV would write her off if she admitted the true number but not if she agreed to lie. As it worked, one can only file it in the bizarre but true column.

Back to true *Vigintiunophilia*, in which there are three stages if true delight is to be attained: prepare, hint, and then out. Or, in the foxy parlance of the vigintiunophile: the beat, the hunt, and the kill. The beat first. All good vigintiunophiles do ample preparation (usually internet research these days) to find suitable coincident or concurrent dates. Suitably armed, then comes the hunt – or the hint, as some call it – wherein dated facts are thrown around like loose grenades with their pins still in. 'Ooh, look, Donovan is doing a concert. Do you remember when he played the Hammersmith Palais, Jean?' If you have chosen wisely, Jean might show a flicker of unease. Do be liberal with your grenades. This is dog whistle *Schadenfreude* at this point: only the person who needs to hear will hear. Hopefully, you will be able to tell when the victim begins to show a little panic. For now it is time for the kill.

It is important that the kill comes in the form of a fact to be deduced, never anything so gauche as an outed age. The killer fact is one that simply can't be missed by all around: we're certainly out of the realms of dog whistle here. We're standing at the back door and shouting 'Here, Rover!' at the top of our voices. The killer fact, then, needs to be pretty obvious. Take this one, I heard the other day: 'Can't believe the Shuttle has finished. Can you remember watching the moon landing on our black and white, Morris?' Vicious. But lovely, see? It's not the age, it's the fact, the comparison date that has killed.

There are some who are trying to work against the ageism status quo, by 'getting the debate out in the open' and other such PC phrases. These people are not to be encouraged. They are merely spoiling everyone's fun. It should also be noted that *Vigintiunophilia reversa* can also be a potent delicacy. This is when a person's youth will work against them in places where age appears to be valued – Russian Presidential elections, those running for Pope, the Arsenal defence, etc – so the outing is done in reverse.

Finally, a recent Channel 21 documentary on the subject, *The Reason of Age*, made a very plausible case to suggest that there is one very high profile vigintiunophile who has gone unnoticed for years, so high up in The Establishment that her black delight has always been hushed up. Think about it: someone who sends telegrams on a daily basis, outing poor innocent centenarians out of supposed 'respect'. I think we should be told.

[viginiti unus, twenty-one]

§

Vilivenophilia: delight in having undersold something wonderful.

A dark art, yes, but surely not one of the darkest. Most people don't consider this a true black delight – perhaps charcoal grey, at worst. What a vilivenophiliac looks for is one of the three great reactions at the point of revelation (that is, the point at which the level and nature of undersell is revealed), namely: the widening of the eyes, the dropping of the jaw, or, if possible, the utterance of a 'Wow!' or similar. Perceived wisdom has it that delights are best taken singly, so as to not detract from one another. Indeed, some psychotherapists believe that cluster undersells can, effectively, become an oversell through sheer volume alone.* The following cluster, for example, is sheer genius when each element is used on its own, but an oversell when taken together: 'Why don't I give you a lift in my jalopy? [Jensen]. I've got a little place just beyond Glastonbury [It's called Devon]. My friend Barry [Barack Obama] will be there too.'

* See article 'Thundersell! Too much, already.' March 1999 edition of *GOING UNDER!* magazine.

[vili, low; vendere, to sell]

§

Vinoptophilia: delight in the display of an invite-only credit card.

Vinoptophilia's roots are lost in the mists of time, but its name suggests it has something to do with the flaunting of fine wines. If practised correctly, this is one of the most subtle philias in the book. Indeed it has to be done subtly or not at all. The chap who mentions his new card all through dinner and annoys the waiter by trying to pay for each course separately is not who is being discussed here. The true vinoptophiliac discreetly takes his card from his wallet at the last moment – preferably while still deep in conversation – and doesn't check the bill. His micro smile, if indeed it is there, is not connected to the flash of recognition, possibly even awe, given off by his dining partners. However, the method of display is all important. In much the same way as the Queen's wave is the result of centuries of tradition, the classic, two-fingered 'cigarette' hold which bears a vinoptophiliac's card aloft to the waiter is very, *very* well practised. Remember, this is their moment.

The card itself, which came in a rhodium box, hand-delivered by limousine (but not until three weeks of 'small tokens of our esteem' such as luxury holidays and hampers had preceded it), is there to be enjoyed. The money transfer side of the transaction is irrelevant. What is relevant is that the bearer has to pay the price of a small London semi as a monthly charge and, as they carelessly let slip, 'the Sultan of Brunei has the one below this.' If possible, the vinoptophiliac times the retrieval of his new pet card from his wallet at precisely the moment when someone else extracts theirs, thus making it appear like a piece of glowing kryptonite against a steaming cowpat. Guess which is which.

[vinum, wine; optimus, best]

Vodeiectophilia: delight in talking without pause.

The massed ranks of vodeiectophiliacs comprise politicians, animal livestock auctioneers, politicians, horse racing commentators, politicians, Alistair Cooke, politicians, monks emerging from a 50-year vow of silence and, finally, politicians. Indeed, it is no coincidence that most private doctors who specialise in the treatment of this 'delight' have a Westminster postcode. Politicians long ago mastered the art of pausing in the… middle of their sentences (before the sense can be understood, and therefore when they were least likely to be interrupted) and then continuing immediately after their sentence has finished, without stopping. This was something they thought was ingenious and guaranteed… to get their point across. But that was before someone invented John Humphrys.

[voce, voice; deiectus, diarrhoea]

Wynnmaphilia: delight while holidaying in the assumption or knowledge that 'the weather back home is awful'.

A typically British delight which gets its name from an old iron-age fort called Wynnman's Hill[*] where it is said it could always be relied upon to be raining. The Brits abroad are the only race guaranteed to be able to suffer from this nauseating philia, because of the near certainty of bad weather back home. Even those native to the plains of Spain do not test quite so positively (or is it negative?) for *Wynnmaphilia*.

For most, this is a mild philia which manifests itself as nothing more than a wry smile to one's loved one, after having glanced upwards at a blue cloudless sky. Moving on up the pleasure curve, many more sufferers will limit themselves to a carefully positioned exclamation mark next to the line 'Wish you were here!' on the postcard home. Others, however, will over indulge in details of how 'the kids have been on the beach EVERY DAY' (capitals, underlined in red) while they themselves – and this is cruel – don't much care for it when it is this stifling and have even had trouble getting through more than a chapter of their holiday book, it's so hot. In this age of email, Skype and IM, the average wynnmaphiliac can indulge in instant gratification, showing the images of themselves, looking for all intents and purposes like a lobster in paradise, pretty much as they happen. How technology spoils us.

[*] Today, Wynnman's Hill is more commonly known as Wimbledon

[Wynnman's Hill, Old Wimbledon]

Index

To delight in,